THE BOOK OF CHALAMET

PESALA BANDARA

CORONET

First published in Great Britain in 2025 by Coronet
An imprint of Hodder & Stoughton Limited
An Hachette UK company

1

A CIP catalogue record for this title is available from the British Library

Hardback ISBN 9781399743938
ebook ISBN 9781399743945

Typeset in Caecilla LT by seagulls.net

Printed and bound in China by C&C Offset Printing Co., Ltd.

Hodder & Stoughton policy is to use papers that are natural, renewable and recyclable products and made from wood grown in sustainable forests. The logging and manufacturing processes are expected to conform to the environmental regulations of the country of origin.

Hodder & Stoughton Limited
Carmelite House
50 Victoria Embankment
London EC4Y 0DZ

The authorised representative in the EEA is Hachette Ireland, 8 Castlecourt Centre, Castleknock Road, Castleknock, Dublin 15, D15 YF6A, Ireland

www.hodder.co.uk

TO WHOM IT CHALAMET CONCERN: THIS LOVING TRIBUTE TO TIMOTHÉE CHALAMET IS NOT OFFICIALLY ENDORSED BY THE MAN HIMSELF – IT IS A FAN'S BOOK FOR FANS THAT CELEBRATES WHAT A WONDERFUL ACTOR AND GUY HE IS ♥

CONTENTS

Introduction

THE KING

WHY WE ALL LOVE TIMOTHÉE CHALAMET

Actor, style-icon, heartthrob – Timothée Chalamet is the man of the moment, following blockbuster success with blockbuster success. But what exactly is it about Timothée that has elevated him to such a unique position in popular culture and won him huge swathes of adoring fans?

He is, of course, one of the leading actors of his generation. He's won many awards, as well as being nominated for an Academy Award, three Golden Globes and two BAFTAs. It was for his breakout role in *Call Me By Your Name* that he received his Oscar nomination for Best Actor, making him the third youngest nominee in that category ever (the youngest since 1939).

He has played varied roles in a thrilling career, from sensitive portrayals of complex characters to those with artful humour. Never willing to settle for what is easy, he is constantly challenging himself with demanding parts – and it turns out he can sing and dance, too!

He is one of the only actors of his generation who is not simply a 'celebrity', but, as *TIME* magazine called him, 'a movie star in the old sense of the word'[1] – one of the very, very few who studios can bet on to launch both a blockbuster franchise and a 'festival' arthouse film. People will pay in their droves to see him in movie theatres – something that is becoming increasingly less common as viewing preferences change and streaming services increase their dominance. He's been compared to the likes of James Dean, River Phoenix and Leonardo DiCaprio.

He is also, undeniably, a 'beautiful boy', with gravity-defying hair and a jawline you could cut your pizza with. His haunting eyes could penetrate your soul and his androgenous good looks have won him admirers from all genders the world over. He's the true modern teen heartthrob who gets rushed at premieres, hounded by the press and has the internet completely obsessed with him (just check out the number of memes!).

But he is so much more than the sum of his parts or simply his looks alone.

Perhaps his appeal lies in his confidence to be unapologetically authentic, embracing fashion choices that are daring and bold. In an age when Hollywood is dominated by macho Marvel superheroes and bulging biceps, Timmy sits apart with his slight frame and impish appeal.

Or perhaps it's in his sweet and humble disposition. With his status and commercial success, it would be easy to stray into self-satisfaction, but in every interview, Timmy expresses genuine gratitude and wide-eyed amazement at the path his life has taken so far. He makes it impossible for us not to love him.

This is a book for fans by a fan. It explores the life, loves and passions of Timothée Chalamet – what makes him tick, how he has followed his dreams and what the principles are that he lives by. We will investigate what his film choices reveal about him, as well as considering the decisions he's taken in his personal life. All the while, we shall explore what lessons we can learn from him, including what it takes to follow your dreams (whatever they may be) and what it means to embrace your authentic self.

At the back of the book, in Chapter Six, you can find quizzes to test your knowledge of all things Chalamet – as well as some other fun and games for a 'Rainy Day' (whether you're in New York or not!). Why not explore what should be the next TC film you watch, depending on your mood? Although, of course, watching any film with him in it is bound to improve any mood!

This book is a true celebration of the man we all adore – Timothée Chalamet.

Chapter One

A WORLD OF YOUR IMAGINATION

HOW TIMOTHÉE CHASED HIS DREAMS

Timothée's career so far has been turbo-charged, as he has achieved roles and accolades at a young age that most actors could only dream of. But when did Timmy discover his destiny, and what path did he take to fulfil his early dreams of becoming an actor? In this chapter we will explore his incredible nascent talent, as well as the drive it took to realise his destiny. We will draw inspiration from his amazing journey and discover what we can learn from him that we can apply to our own lives and dreams, whatever they might look like.

WRITTEN IN THE STARS

Timothée Hal Chalamet was born on 27 December 1995, in New York City. This just happens to make him a Capricorn. But what does his star sign reveal about him?

The last earth sign of the zodiac, Capricorn is characterised by the goat (which, as we all know, stands for 'greatest of all time' – something TC is certainly on track to becoming!). Capricorns are known to be powerful, ambitious and resilient. Just like goats, which are skilled at navigating tricky terrains and steadily moving onward, Capricorns can push through adversity to achieve their long-term goals. They don't like to be bogged down by unnecessary details – they keep their eyes on the prize, retain perspective and, although some think they can be perceived as cold or unemotional, they're really just focused. They can also be very creative and visionary, particularly relevant for Timothée, whose Capricorn stellium is concentrated in the fifth house. We can certainly assume Timmy has harnessed the power of his sign to achieve the incredible career he has had so far – he is very strategic about the roles he takes and has compared his acting career to a marathon rather than a sprint[1] – something he admits is hard in a culture of instant gratification.

As well as their confidence and ambition, Capricorns are also known to be grounded and practical, with a calming presence that makes others feel comfortable with them. They're selective about who they let into their lives but are loyal friends to those that do make the cut.

That said, they certainly have a rebellious and untamed streak! They have been said to age backwards, with a Benjamin Button-esque ability to seem more playful and youthful as they get older. Considering Timothée Chalamet can still play a young boy in his late twenties, that certainly rings true! They have also been called mischievous troublemakers (in Tarot, the devil card represents Capricorn), and Timmy certainly has a sense of mischief. He is often involved in pranks with co-stars (although often he is the target of those pranks!), but as a child sometimes these pranks went sideways – in an interview on *The Ellen DeGeneres Show* in 2019, he confessed to an occasion when he hugely embarrassed his mum. They were on a cruise ship, and after a shower she stepped out briefly onto their balcony and he locked her out as a joke. She was fully naked, but at that point no one would have been able to see her – but then Timmy realised he couldn't find the key card to let her back in! He ran the length of the ship a few times to find someone to help, in floods of tears, by which time the ship had arrived in the port and his mum was trying her best to cover herself up! A kind boy at heart, though, Timmy was in such a state by this point, she didn't even bother scolding him.[2]

Romantically speaking, Capricorns are said to be seeking an anchor – they're often incredibly busy, so need someone steady and loyal. Virgo and Taurus can be compatible as fellow earth signs, but the water signs Pisces, Scorpio and Cancer can be a wonderful fit with Capricorn, bringing sensitivity and compassion to the relationship.

Other hardworking, visionary Capricorns include Dolly Parton, Lin-Manuel Miranda, Michelle Obama and John Legend – all known for their dedication, sophistication and immense talent – just like our Timothée.

IMMERSED IN A WORLD OF YOUR IMAGINATION

TC was born into a creative family, so was surrounded by inspiration from a very young age. His mother, Nicole Flender, had majored in dance at LaGuardia High School of Music & Art and Performing Arts (sometimes known as the 'Fame School'), which was the same school that Timothée and his sister Pauline (who is four years older than him) attended many years later. Nicole went on to become a performer on Broadway and then a dance teacher, and met Timmy's father, Marc Chalamet, when he was on a business trip to NYC for the French newspaper *Le Parisien*.

This dual perspective from his parents from the worlds of showbusiness and the media was clearly very useful for Tim when setting out on his own career in acting. Indeed, his mum has been a vocal advocate for child actors' rights, as well as better working conditions for stage actors. She was elected to the Actors' Equity Association, negotiating for the 50,000 stage actors represented by the union. Other creative influences on Timmy include a famous aunt and uncle in writer/producers Amy Lippman and Rodman Flender, as well as a screenwriter maternal grandfather!

Timothée grew up in the federally subsidised artists' building Manhattan Plaza in the Hell's Kitchen district of New York City – under its Section 8 federal funding, the building must have 70 per cent of tenants from fields in the performing arts. The other 30 per cent can be decided at its discretion, but it chooses to select the elderly and neighbourhood residents. Many successful artists have called it home at some point or another, including Alicia Keys and Larry David.

Nicole didn't miss out on opportunities to inspire her kids' creativity – 'I took them to see many different plays and musicals when they were growing up, and I think seeing certain performances influenced them. The productions they've seen and even growing up in New York has informed who they are today,' she said in an interview with the *Guardian*.[3] She noted that her son's favourite performance was *Slava's Snowshow*, a magical production that completely wowed him.

The creative exposure from a young age certainly provided a fertile breeding ground for the Chalamet family – Tim's sister is a successful actress in her own right, with credits including *The Secret Lives of College Girls* and *The King of Staten Island*. She has described how, growing up in the Manhattan Plaza, it was common to hear neighbours singing opera or playing piano in the hours that were dedicated for residents to rehearse. In an interview with *Vanity Fair*, she said that a love of art 'was in my family, and it was also really in the building in which I grew up. It was always there.'[4] Apparently, she tried to escape the performing arts, in what she describes as her 'rebellious phase' towards her upbringing. But, despite being determined to become a lawyer, she couldn't escape the pull of acting and directing. A pull that her brother most certainly knew all too well.

THE FRENCH DISPATCH

Timmy has also spoken a lot about how he's been influenced by his French heritage. Because of his dad, he is bilingual and has dual citizenship. Growing up, he spent many summers with his grandparents in a small French village near Lyon called Le Chambon-sur-Lignon. Although he has said that these two very different environments led to some confusion around his identity (see Chapter Five), ultimately embracing both his French and American sides led to a more fluid sense of himself that is not so easy to categorise.

If there could be anything hotter than Timmy Chalamet speaking English, it would surely be him speaking to you in French, so here are some useful phrases in the language of love (which you could either try on the object of your affection, or perhaps just imagine Timmy saying them to you):

- *J'adore ton sourire* – I love your smile
- *Tu as de beaux yeux* – You have beautiful eyes
- *Je veux être avec toi* – I want to be with you
- *Tu es l'homme/la femme de mes rêves* – You are the man/woman of my dreams

- *Tu es l'amour de ma vie* – You're the love of my life
- *Je t'ai dans la peau* – I've got you under my skin
- *Je t'aimerai jusqu'à mon dernier souffle* – I will love you until my last breath
- *Sans toi, je ne suis rien* – Without you, I am nothing
- *Est-ce que tu veux sortir avec moi?* – Will you go out with me?
- *Pour toi, bébé, je décrocherai la lune* – For you, baby, I'll get the moon
- *Tes yeux sont comme des étoiles* – Your eyes are like stars
- *J'aimerais être une de tes larmes pour naître dans tes yeux, vivre sur tes joues et mourir sur tes lèvres* – I'd like to be one of your tears to be born in your eyes, live on your cheeks and die on your lips

FINDING HIS DREAM

Although Timothée's mum, Nicole Flender, was certainly hopeful her kids would find their way to the performing arts, she never pushed them to pursue that career path. 'I planted seeds,' she has said, 'and our lifestyle really inspired those interests, but they always had control of their careers. I was encouraging, you know, but I wasn't like, "You better get this job."'[5] Which is certainly fortunate, as it's unlikely Tim would have been able to keep his feet on the ground had he not

approached his career with a genuine enthusiasm and without undue pressure. Many a young performer has had their joy in acting quashed by a tiger-parent!

In kindergarten, Timmy started acting in commercials but without great interest. In fact, he found them decidedly boring. 'I didn't enjoy just standing around smiling for five hours in front of a camera. It's all so fake,' Timothée later recalled.[6] Instead, growing up, Timothée was set on becoming a sports star like football player Lionel Messi or basketball legend LeBron James.[7]

But that all changed when Timothée went to see Christopher Nolan's *The Dark Knight* with his family when he was 12 years old. Timothée was so impressed and overwhelmed by Heath Ledger's performance as the Joker – taking that famous role and making it entirely his own with his odd quirks and speech patterns – that he left the cinema determined to pursue acting. 'I left that theatre a changed man, and I'm serious about that,' Timothée said. 'Heath Ledger's performance in that film was visceral and viral to me, and I now had the acting bug.'[8]

He also realised in middle school – when he was taken on for the selective Delta programme at MS 54 Booker T. Washington Middle School – how important it was to have a creative outlet. This was something he was severely lacking within the school's academically rigorous environment, and he has said this made him miserable at the time.

One year later, Timothée was accepted at Fiorello H. LaGuardia High School of Music & Art and Performing Arts in New York, which is famed for producing generations of talented actors. Timothée was initially rejected by the competitive school, which includes stars like Nicki Minaj, Robert De Niro and Jennifer Aniston among its notable alumni. But LaGuardia's drama teacher Harry Shifman saw something in Timothée. Shifman gave the then-13-year-old Timothée the highest score he had ever doled out in an acting audition and pushed for the 'brilliant' teen to be accepted into the school.[9] I bet that teacher is pretty pleased with his talent-spotting abilities now he's been proved right on the button! Give that guy a raise!

Timothée fell in love with the craft of acting at LaGuardia. He described the moment he first realised that 'the invincible Messis and LeBrons weren't as interesting to me as the artists who were vulnerable for a living — the Heath Ledgers, the Joaquin Phoenixes'.[10]

He later told the Columbia University student newspaper that LaGuardia changed a lot for him, and he no longer regarded acting as 'machine of fakeness'.[11] It opened his eyes to the truth and craft of acting, what it can reveal about ourselves, and that it is anything but fake. It was here that he started to truly dream and to believe that his dream could become a reality. In these years he took huge inspiration from other great actors – a particular performance of note was seeing Philip Seymour Hoffman as Willy Loman in the Broadway production of *Death of a Salesman*.

During high school Timothée stared in the musicals *Cabaret* and *Sweet Charity*. Many TC fans are desperate to see him revisit his role as the Emcee in the former, a role tailor-made for him – or so anyone who has seen him twirling his stick and dancing with his top hat in *Wonka* would assume! The Emcee is also famously a very fluid, mischievous character. It would be interesting to know how much playing that character has informed his acting and persona to date – particularly leaning into the gender-non-conforming aspects of the role and his comedic flourishes. Hopefully Timmy fans may one day get the chance to see him reprise it!

Timothée has described the thrill he found when he started acting, and continues to feel every time he gets on stage or behind the camera. Quite the opposite of the 'fakeness' he once thought acting involved, he has said it awakens hidden parts of him and shakes them loose: 'I think that whatever bone gets electrified when I act, there's always a feeling that I'm a little bit out of my depth or out of control.'[12] He knows that staying in your safe space is never going to allow for true creativity or dynamic performances – and would be very boring! This uncertainty seems like a welcome release.

FINDING YOUR DREAM

Timothée was very lucky that his dream was closely aligned to the future his mother had hoped for him and, in many ways, the path life led him to. While not quite a nepo-baby – and clearly immensely talented – he was certainly in an environment that supported and enabled the career he chose for himself. What happened next was the result of his hard work, vision and commitment to his future. But how do we discover what our dream is if it is not so obvious to us from a young age? Here are some tips to help you determine what it is you want to do with your life:

1 **Consider your values.** Timmy has often aligned the roles he's taken with the values that are most important to him, including promoting messages to break the taboo around addiction (*Beautiful Boy*) and LGBTQ+ acceptance (*Call My By Your Name*) (see Chapter Five for a full exploration of the causes Timmy cares most about). But it goes further than the roles he's played, as his whole career path tells us what is important to Timmy. He only really considered acting when, at LaGuardia, he came to understand what art was really all about – helping us to process important truths about life. When trying to identify what dream you want to follow in your life, think about your own core values and factor them into your decision-making process. Freedom and autonomy? Representation? Equality? Community? Authenticity? Integrity? Write them down!

2 **Identify your needs.** What are your non-negotiables when it comes to how you spend your time? What is crucial for your own wellbeing? Is it financial freedom? A healthy work–life balance? Lots of time spent outdoors or being active? Being able to set your own schedule? Obviously, there is usually some compromise required when it comes to the reality of the working world, but it's important to consider your priorities and parameters when framing what your dream could be. These may shift over time – Timmy didn't date for a while when focusing on getting his career started – but creative freedom and finding meaning were clearly big ones for Timmy that he has stuck by at every step.

3 **List your skills.** You should start by writing down absolutely everything you're good at, whether or not you think these talents will naturally lead to a career or life goal. You never know what could be transferrable! Can you speak a foreign language, like Timmy? Do you have an eye for fashion, or can you make people laugh? Are you good with kids or animals? Are you good at video games or baking? These skills could be things you might put on a CV, but they certainly don't have to be – you never know which talent might be useful to someone or could be something you might get paid for!

4 **What are your greatest achievements so far?** And, no, it doesn't have to be something as obvious as an award (not all of us have an Oscar nomination to point to). What are you most proud of? Could it be helping someone else through an exam? Keeping on with something even though it was really hard? Battling demons of your own? Or maybe it was something creative, like decorating your living room on a tight budget. List anything that comes to mind.

5 **What brings you joy?** Start by listing things that are fun for you, such as playing football or going to the theatre. Tim made silly videos as a teenager – such as his infamous 'statistics' rap (google it!) – where he clearly had fun, and which pointed to his love of performing. But these can also be things that make you feel content or valued, such as visiting an elderly neighbour or baking for friends. Wouldn't it be great to be able to scale up something you love and turn it into a career?

6 **What makes you unhappy?** What drains your energy or negatively affects your mental health? Too much time alone? Too much time in company? Answering to someone else? Pressure? It's worth keeping these things in mind when considering what you want to do, or at least exploring whether these factors could be mitigated.

7 **If you didn't have to consider limitations, what would you do?** Note down the ideas that immediately come to mind, not worrying about distance, dependants, money or anything else. Timmy was lucky to have identified his dream so young when he didn't really have anything huge to factor in – although, as we'll see in the next section, he did have to set his education aside to pursue acting. You may have major factors that you will have to consider at some point, but starting from this place of complete freedom might help you realise what you may be willing to sacrifice in the name of your dreams.

Having worked through this process, you can start thinking more laterally about what your true dream might be. Have you identified any passions that could be turned into a career or at least used within it? Could a love of shopping be turned into a personal shopping business? Or might you want to think about becoming a fashion influencer? If you love playing football but aren't going to be able to pursue it professionally, might you want to start coaching kids instead? If you love reading, how about book publishing? Think how much happier you could be doing something you really love!

STAYING ON THE PATH

The trickiest moment for Timmy so far came after he enrolled in Columbia University. He had struggled academically in middle school, and then found the rigorous environment at Columbia particularly hard to navigate. He had already found his calling and his heart just wasn't in academia at that point – in his words, he 'floundered'.[13]

Rather than being disheartened at struggling in one area of his life, however, he decided to commit fully to his dream of acting instead, saying, 'Now that my foot is in the door, I'm locked and loaded. I'm focused.'[14] But his mum was against his decision! She had attended Yale and wanted her son to have some qualifications to fall back on if acting didn't work out. Fortunately, it very much did work out. As she later said, admitting that her son made the right call, 'We didn't know that he was going to become Timothée Chalamet!'[15]

TIPS FROM TIMOTHÉE

- **Surround yourself with people who inspire you.** We can't all have TC's good fortune and be born into a family of artists, but we can find like-minded people who we can learn from, who can inspire us and who we can collaborate with. Whatever our passion, there's always a club to join or individuals to connect with, even if it's just online. Although there are exceptions, most of us don't find true creativity in a vacuum.

ABSOLUT
MPH()MANIAC
ELYX

- **Have fun!** If you watch Lil Timmy Tim's school rap video on statistics (a project for which he amazingly only got a D!), you'll see that he didn't take himself too seriously and always enjoyed playing around with different things. While you may feel very deeply about your passion or career, finding the fun will often free you up and give you energy to pursue your dreams.
- **Don't be afraid to dream big.** Ambition is an incredibly positive attribute if you're happy to work hard to get where you want to go. Set your eyes on the prize.
- **Love what you do (even if not all the time).** Timmy was a poor student when he was feeling uninspired at middle school, but finding the thing that made his soul light up made a world of difference.
- **It's a marathon, not a sprint.** Like any good Capricorn, TC knew a long time ago what he wanted to do with his life and has played a very strategic game to get where he is today, taking the roles that would best showcase his talent without allowing him to be typecast. We can learn a lot from his forward-planning and commitment to his vision.
- **The right training is invaluable.** While a number of actors have broken through in Hollywood with little or even no formal training, if there is an opportunity to learn from experts in their field, that can't be a bad thing – it certainly worked for Tim! Whatever your chosen career, it is always useful to consider what options are open to you that

might help you excel, whether that's academic learning, mentorship, apprenticeship or any other kind of training.

* **Stay true to yourself.** See Chapter Five for a thorough exploration of Timothée's commitment to authenticity, but it is clear from every interview what a genuine guy he is. Keeping your feet on the ground and not losing sight of what is important to you will keep you moving on the right path.

* **It's OK to make mistakes.** As Timmy said himself, 'I know from working on a movie that if a scene goes wrong, and there's laughter on set, it loosens you up for the next take, it's better than protecting yourself and getting lost in your head.'[16] It's much better to take risks and be brave than to hold back and never try.

* **Take strength from those who love you.** Timmy is fortunate to be from a loving family who have always supported his dreams and helped him to fulfil them – and he has kept them close by, often taking them to awards shows and industry events. He has also always supported the careers of those he loves, whether that's raving about the work of one of his inspirations or telling people to go and see his sister's movie! Of course, not everyone is gifted with such a tight-knit, supportive family, so finding your tribe may take more effort and time – but it's always worth it. Having a solid network of friends and family gives a powerful foundation on which to build your dreams.

Chapter Two

INTERSTELLAR CAREER

THE ROLES THAT MADE THE MAN

With a career that includes playing an angsty teenage cannibal, an eccentric chocolatier and a Fremen leader who can control a sandworm like nobody's business, Timothée Chalamet is a bona fide movie star.

Despite still being so young, Timothée has become one of the most in-demand actors in Hollywood and a household name who can sell out cinemas. Yet he has accomplished this in the most unconventional way.

When Timothée was catapulted to widespread fame and mainstream heartthrob status with his iconic role as Elio Perlman in *Call Me By Your Name*, the then-21-year-old actor could have followed a very conventional and predictable path to becoming a major movie star. After the critical acclaim of *Call Me By Your Name*, most young actors would have been quickly swept up into major studio projects and franchises. However, Timothée did the complete opposite.

He bided his time in the wake of the unexpected success of *Call Me By Your Name*, and then took a curated and highly selective approach to his career, going for offbeat and eclectic roles in independent and arthouse films such as *Beautiful Boy* and *Lady Bird*.

And while most A-listers in his position would have refused to settle for anything less than a lead role in a movie, Timothée has been more than happy to opt for a supporting role in a film on numerous occasions. He had no problem playing a supporting role as Laurie to the female leads in Greta Gerwig's

Little Women – or taking a small but memorable role as Jennifer Lawrence's shoplifting skater boyfriend Yule among a star-studded ensemble cast in *Don't Look Up*.

Furthermore, before playing Paul Atreides in *Dune*, Timothée had never even starred in a massive studio blockbuster movie.

For Timothée, the only thing that has ever seemed to matter above all else was making important and great films that audiences can truly care about. When he was asked about how he saw his multifaceted career evolving during a press conference for *Bones and All*, Timothée had a simple answer. 'I want to make movies that matter and speak to people,' he said. 'I think it's the role of the artist to shine a light on what's going on.'[1]

Alongside his once-in-a-generation talent, it has been this thoughtful, sensitive and deliberate approach to his career that has made Timothée the beloved movie star he is today. Timothée has not only consistently earned critical praise with his roles, but he also broke box-office records when he starred in *Wonka* and *Dune: Part Two* in 2024. So, how did Timothée become one of Hollywood's foremost actors? And what can we learn from his story? Let's take a look at his journey from arthouse actor to heartthrob and box-office darling.

THE ACTING BUG (2007–2008)

Films include: *Clown*, *Sweet Tooth*

Notable awards: None

While studying at LaGuardia, Timothée truly caught the acting bug and starred in several school theatre productions. Initially, he failed to crack the lead role in the school's musical productions, with that coveted spot always going to his classmate, the soon-to-be-famous actor Ansel Elgort.[2] But that didn't deter Timothée. He continued to work hard at LaGuardia and it wouldn't be long until he landed his first real acting credits.

These included roles in two short horror films called *Sweet Tooth* and *Clown*. In *Clown*, he played a child kidnapped by circus clowns in the 1880s. Meanwhile, in *Sweet Tooth*, he took on the role of a young boy called Samuel who hides in the garden of an isolated cottage with his sister.

FIRST REAL ROLES (2009–2013)

Films include: *Loving Leah*

Notable awards: Screen Actors Guild Award nomination for Best Cast in a Drama Series for *Homeland*

In 2009, Timothée scored his first proper acting job with a brief appearance in the long-running television crime drama *Law & Order*. He made a cameo as a boy who is later found dead in his home alongside his housekeeper. *Law & Order* and its many spin-offs has a reputation for giving future major actors their first shot in the entertainment industry. Timothée later acknowledged this opportunity in an interview with Ellen DeGeneres: '*Law & Order* is the mothership … that gives everybody their start in acting.'[3] And sure enough, a few months later, Timothée would land his next acting job – a minor role in the TV movie *Loving Leah*.

In 2011, Tim went on to make his stage debut as a sexually curious 12-year-old boy in the off-Broadway play *The Talls*. And in 2012, Timothée would land a recurring role as awkward teen Luke in the television drama *Royal Pains*. His run lasted for four episodes.

Later that year, Timothée landed a prominent role in the hit television show *Homeland* as the vice president's son, Finn Walden. The role would help jumpstart Timothée's career and get him noticed by viewers. Initially, Timmy was only meant to appear in one episode of *Homeland*, but the role was expanded across the entire second season of the show. Timmy was well received for his turn as the troublemaking Finn. Along with the rest of the actors in *Homeland*, Timothée was nominated for a Screen Actors Guild Award for Best Cast in a Drama Series – his first major nomination.

Timothée had to miss half of his senior year at LaGuardia to appear in *Homeland*.[4] But he still managed to graduate from high school on time in 2013 and enrolled at Columbia University to study cultural anthropology.

THE BIG BREAK THAT WASN'T (2014)

Films include: *Interstellar, Men, Women & Children, Worst Friends*

Notable awards: None

In 2014, Timothée landed a minor role in the drama *Men, Women & Children* alongside an A-list cast that included Adam Sandler and Jennifer Garner. He also got a small part in the dark comedy *Worst Friends*.

That same year, however, Timothée landed a seemingly career-making role in the Christopher Nolan film *Interstellar*. Nolan cast Timothée as Tom Cooper, the teenage son of NASA pilot Joseph Cooper, played by Matthew McConaughey. Timothée was positive that his performance in *Interstellar* would serve as a breakout role for him and a catalyst for his career as a movie star. Certain that his ascent to Hollywood stardom was imminent, Timothée dropped out of Columbia University after filming *Interstellar* to pursue acting full-time and began renting his own apartment in the Bronx, New York.[5]

However, when Timothée went to the *Interstellar* premiere and watched the film, he discovered that his role was not as crucial as he had anticipated. His emotional monologue scene had been significantly cut and Timothée returned home from the *Interstellar* screening in tears. While he loved the final film, he 'wept for an hour' after the premiere because he expected his role in the sci-fi film to be bigger.[6]

D'S NEXT STEP WILL BE OUR GREATES
A FILM BY CHRISTOPHER NOLAN
RSTELL
WARNER BROS. PICTURES PRESENT
MATTHEW McCONAUGHEY
MICHAEL CAINE

Interstellar went on to become one of the highest-grossing films of 2014, but it wasn't the breakthrough role Timothée hoped it would be for him.

Now, he found himself broke and emotionally struggling in ways he hadn't expected.[7] Looking back on this challenging time after *Interstellar*, Timothée called it 'the scariest year of my life'.[8]

RISING STAR (2015–2016)

Films include: *Miss Stevens*, *Love the Coopers*, *One & Two*, *The Adderall Diaries*

Notable awards: Lucille Lortel Award for Outstanding Lead Actor in a Play and a nomination for the Drama League Award for Distinguished Performance

Timothée had serious financial problems after *Interstellar* – the role he had imagined would be his career breakout. With no upcoming acting jobs on the horizon, Timothée auditioned constantly but he faced rejections at every turn. Timothée says he auditioned for the *Spider-Man* films, Tim Burton's *Miss Peregrine's Home for Peculiar Children*, and the Stephen Hawking biopic *The Theory of Everything*, among numerous other projects, but didn't get booked for a single part.[9] Once, he remembers rehearsing for an entire week for an audition for the film *The Neon Demon* but never even getting a response from the casting directors.[10] With the constant rejections coming at him, Timothée felt like giving up and couldn't even face going to the cinema to watch movies any more as it hurt too much.[11]

Eventually, though, after a tumultuous period of zero success, Timothée started getting hired for roles. In 2015, he earned a minor role as Diane Keaton and John Goodman's teenage grandson in the Christmas comedy *Love the Coopers*. Timothée's next role would see him play the younger version of James Franco's character in *The Adderall Diaries*. He then starred alongside Kiernan Shipka in the fantasy thriller *One & Two* as a teenager with special powers who lives isolated from the rest of the world.

However, in 2016, Timothée's career would really start to blossom. The then-20-year-old would play a volatile student who finds his poetic purpose at a private school in a production of *The Prodigal Son* at the Manhattan Theatre Club. Timothée's performance was praised and critics began to notice his talent, dubbing him 'a rising star' for the first time.[12] To crown this achievement, he then won the Lucille Lortel Award for Outstanding Lead Actor in a Play, as well as a nomination for the Drama League Award for Distinguished Performance.

Timothée would then play gifted but disturbed school student Billy who forms a bond with his high-school teacher in the movie *Miss Stevens*, and more critical success would follow. Film critics were impressed by Timothée's striking performance. The *New York Times* compared him to a younger James Dean.[13] And after watching *Miss Stevens*, *Vulture* film critic Alison Willmore was left 'convinced' that 'Timothée

Chalamet was going to be a movie star'.[14] Things were looking up for Timothée, but his breakthrough proper would happen the following year.

TIMOTHÉE THE ARTHROB (2017)

Films include: *Call Me By Your Name*, *Hot Summer Nights*

Notable awards: Academy Award nomination for Best Actor and a Golden Globe nomination for Best Actor in a Motion Picture (Drama) for *Call Me By Your Name*

Timothée had been tentatively attached to star in Luca Guadagnino's coming-of-age movie *Call Me By Your Name* for three years before shooting finally began in northern Italy in 2016. Timmy was set to play 17-year-old Elio Perlman who falls in love with 24-year-old Oliver, who is hired as his father's research assistant. To prepare for the role, Timothée spent six weeks learning Italian and taking daily piano and guitar lessons before filming started on the low-budget indie flick.[15]

When *Call Me By Your Name* was released in 2017, it immediately propelled Timothée to superstardom and unexpectedly established him as a heartthrob (or, more accurately, an 'artthrob')[16] overnight. Timothée's impeccable performance as the young and vulnerable Elio and his heartbreaking portrayal of first love in *Call Me By Your Name* was applauded by critics and audiences alike. For his performance, Timothée was nominated for an Academy Award

for Best Actor – becoming the youngest nominee to achieve this since 1939. Timothée was also nominated for a Golden Globe Award and a Screen Actors Guild Award for his turn in *Call Me By Your Name*, among numerous other accolades.

Moreover, Chalamet's breakthrough performance (bolstered by a scene involving a peach!) solidified his status as cinema's new sweet, sensitive heartthrob and kicked off an online fandom known as 'Chalamania'.

Hot Summer Nights, which was shot long before Timothée filmed *Call Me By Your Name*, was also released in cinemas a few months later.[17] In *Hot Summer Nights*, he played a teenage boy who becomes entangled in the drugs trade and was once again praised for his performance in the film.

Timothée's reputation as the internet's pre-eminent heartthrob was sealed. To this day, Timothée believes he would never have had such a glittering career if Guadagnino had not cast him in *Call Me By Your Name*.[18] After years of casting calls and screen tests, Timothée hardly ever had to audition for another project again following the success of the movie.[19]

Timothée was becoming a sought-after actor in Hollywood, and it was expected that he would only be starring in major studio movies henceforth – but this couldn't have been more wrong. Timothée was now going to be highly selective and discerning about the projects he took on.

INDIE ICON (2017–2018)

Films include: *Lady Bird*, *Beautiful Boy*, *Hostiles*

Notable awards: Golden Globe nomination for Best Supporting Actor for *Beautiful Boy* and a Teen Choice nomination for Movie Actor for *Lady Bird*

Timothée followed up his breakout role in *Call Me By Your Name* with a string of impressive performances in independent movies. Rather than immediately leaping at the opportunity to star in a mainstream movie, Timothée selected projects based on their artistic merit instead of their box-office potential. And he also selected characters that showed a different side to his romantic appeal in *Call Me By Your Name*.

In 2017, Timothée took a supporting role opposite Saoirse Ronan (whom he would go on to work with again and again!) in Greta Gerwig's *Lady Bird*. Timothée gave a hilarious performance as Christine's pretentious, dirtbag boyfriend. In the role, he subverted his newly cemented heartthrob status. He also appeared in a scene-stealing cameo as French private Philippe Dejardin alongside Christian Bale in the western drama *Hostiles*.

In 2018, Timothée starred in *Beautiful Boy*, which chronicles a family's struggle as their son battles with substance abuse.

Tim played Steve Carell's son Nic, who grapples with an addiction to hard drugs. Timothée spent time with patients in rehab and lost 18lbs to prepare for the role.[20] He received widespread critical acclaim for his unflinching performance and earned a nomination for a Golden Globe Award for Best Supporting Actor for the role, among several other accolades. Timothée was quickly proving himself to be an icon of indie cinema.

HIGHS AND LOWS (2019)

Films include: *A Rainy Day in New York*, *The King*, *Little Women*

Notable awards: Critics Choice Award Nomination for Best Cast for *Little Women*

After a period of critical acclaim in his professional career, Timothée was about to face his first set of creative challenges. In 2019, he starred in Woody Allen's romantic comedy *A Rainy Day in New York* alongside Selena Gomez. While Timmy received praise for his comedic performance, the film was immediately a subject of controversy.

The production of *A Rainy Day in New York* came at the height of the #MeToo movement and there was a resurgence of interest around the historic sexual abuse allegations surrounding the film's director Allen (which he has denied). In light of these allegations, distributor Amazon Studios cancelled the movie's release. Timothée responded to the scandal by expressing remorse for taking a role in Allen's movie. But he also decided

to take an action that spoke louder than words and donated his wages from *A Rainy Day in New York* to Time's Up and other charities. 'I don't want to profit from my work on the film,' he wrote in an Instagram post.[21]

Later that year, Timothée gave a compelling lead performance as King Henry V of England in *The King*. He chopped his signature luscious curls into a bowl cut to play the unlikeable fifteenth-century monarch – in a role that swung even further from the pretty-boy archetype he was famed for. He also starred in a supporting role as the lovable Laurie in *Little Women* – collaborating with *Lady Bird* director Greta Gerwig and *Lady Bird* co-star Saoirse Ronan again. Numerous critics hailed Tim's performance as Laurie as perfect casting, agreeing that 'it's difficult to imagine anyone better than Chalamet' in the role.[22]

DID YOU KNOW? Timothée and Saoirse were meant to make a cameo on Greta Gerwig's *Barbie*, but sadly, the actors couldn't make it happen with their schedules. Timothée mused that he could have starred as a 'reject French' Ken![23]

A BLOCKBUSTER STAR IS BORN (2021)

Films include: *Dune*, *The French Dispatch*, *Don't Look Up*

Notable awards: MTV Movie Award nomination for Best Actor in *Dune* and a Screen Actors Guild Award nomination for Outstanding Performance by a Cast in *Don't Look Up*

Next, TC would take on a project that would undoubtedly be the most significant and high-profile role of his career to date. Up until this point, Timothée had been a veteran of small-budget indie films and likely eschewed the lucrative offers that must have been coming his way.

But when director Denis Villeneuve began the casting process for his big-budget movie adaption of the sci-fi classic *Dune*, based on the novel by Frank Herbert, there was only one actor he wanted to play the superhuman heir Paul Atreides … and that was Timothée Chalamet, of course! Villeneuve was convinced that Timothée was the only young actor who had the emotional intelligence and unrivalled talent to take on the lead role. 'We didn't have a Plan B,' Villeneuve recalled. 'Honestly, if he said no, I don't know what I would have done. There would be no *Dune* maybe.'[24]

Thankfully, Timothée was keen to work with the influential director and felt confident in Villeneuve's epic vision for the film.[25] He was the first actor to be cast in *Dune* before the likes of Zendaya and Jason Momoa joined the project. Never having embarked on a lead role in a special-effects-laden blockbuster movie before, Timothée admits he was 'blindsided' by the scale of the production for *Dune*.[26] He spent months filming in scorching-hot temperatures in the Wadi Rum desert in Jordan. But, Timothée said, the gruelling shoot allowed him to immerse himself in the character of Paul even more.

When *Dune* was released in 2021, it was a huge box-office smash hit that went on to win six Academy Awards. It was not only beloved by audiences; the film was also well received by critics – many of whom praised Timothée's standout performance among the ensemble cast. 'Simply put, this was the honour of a lifetime for me,' Timmy said at the time of *Dune*'s premiere. 'I hope we get to do a second one. It would be a dream.'[27] Sure enough, following the first film's success, Villeneuve quickly received the green light for the sequel, *Dune: Part Two*.[28]

While Timothée became a multiplex star with *Dune* in 2021, he never forgot his arthouse roots. In the same year, he starred in a supporting role as the self-serious student revolutionary leader Zeffirelli in Wes Anderson's *The French Dispatch* (his third film with Saoirse Ronan). Anderson wrote the role with Timmy in mind.[29] The director is known for recasting the same actors in his films, and so Wes Anderson regulars such as Bill Murray and Tilda Swinton starred in *The French Dispatch*. But Timothée was a total newcomer on Anderson's set, and he took this rare opportunity seriously. He prepared intensely and watched all of Anderson's movies before accepting the role of Zeffirelli.[30] Timmy was praised for his charming performance in the film.

Timothée also took another supporting role in the political satire *Don't Look Up*, alongside a star-studded cast that included Hollywood heavyweights Leonardo DiCaprio and Meryl Streep. Timothée showcased his comedic prowess in his brief appearance as a social rebel. The movie also became the second-most-watched movie of all time on streaming platform Netflix.

ESTABLISHED LEADING MAN (2022–2024)

Films include: *Wonka*, *Dune: Part Two*, *Bones and All*

Notable awards: Golden Globe Award nomination for Best Actor in a Motion Picture (Musical or Comedy) for *Wonka*

By 2022, Timothée had established himself as one of the most talented and bankable stars in Hollywood, but he was about to make box-office history two years later.

First, he reunited with *Call Me By Your Name* director Luca Guadagnino in the film *Bones and All*. Timothée delivered a commanding performance as a young cannibal who falls in love. In an end-of-year review of *Bones and All*, *Hollywood Reporter* critic Jon Frosch called Timmy 'the best actor of his generation' and said that audiences 'may be at a point where we're taking for granted how good he is'.[31] Tim also served as a producer on the film, something that he hopes to do on future film projects, too.[32]

Then, in 2023, Timothée stepped away from the prestigious movies he was known for and starred as the younger version of Roald Dahl's chocolatier Willy Wonka in the musical fantasy film *Wonka*. Timmy says he loved the idea of making a fun movie that was different to anything he had done before. 'To work on something that will have an uncynical young audience, that was just a big joy. That's why I was drawn to it,' he said of *Wonka*.[33]

Wonka director Paul King offered the part to Timothée with no audition after seeing his vocal skills in his high-school musical performances on YouTube (statistics, anyone?).[34] But Timothée still did intense vocal training every day for eight weeks before filming began on *Wonka*.[35]

Initially, Timothée's casting in *Wonka* was met with doubts – some critics suggested that the film was an unnecessary remake of the original 1971 film *Willy Wonka & the Chocolate Factory*.[36] However, Timmy proved the doubters wrong and charmed critics with his heartwarming performance.

Wonka was also a commercial success, grossing $632 million worldwide.

Then, in early 2024, Timothée's box-office domination hit fever pitch when he starred in the highly anticipated sequel *Dune: Part Two*. The follow-up to *Dune* grossed over $712 million worldwide and broke several box-office records. Furthermore, with the success of *Wonka* and *Dune: Part Two*, Timothée achieved something that no actor had done in a long time. He became the first actor in over four decades to star in the top-two domestic-grossing films over a span of eight months – again breaking box-office records.[37]

WHAT'S NEXT? At the time of writing, Timothée is signed on to produce and star as Bob Dylan in the forthcoming biopic *A Complete Unknown*. Timothée will do all his own singing in the movie.[38] He is also set to star in and produce *Marty Supreme*, an original movie inspired by professional ping pong player Marty Reisman.[39] And, of course, *Dune: Part Three* is confirmed as being in development after the wild success of *Dune: Part Two*.[40]

DO LOOK UP

Timothée has looked up to certain actors all his life and even had the opportunity to work with some of his heroes. Here are a few of the stars who have inspired Timothée in his career.

- **STEVE CARELL:** Timothée is a huge fan of *The Office* and says it is his favourite TV show ever.[41] So he was nervous and excited to work alongside the show's lead star Steve Carell in *Beautiful Boy*.[42] Timothée says that he learned so much from Carell, especially in terms of 'his professionalism and the way he carries himself as a man'.[43]
- **LEONARDO DICAPRIO:** Timothée is often compared to Leonardo DiCaprio in terms of their acting talent, and they got the opportunity to work together on *Don't Look Up*. Timothée revealed that DiCaprio gave him some simple career advice on set: 'No hard drugs and no superhero movies!'[44]

* **JOAQUIN PHOENIX:** Timothée says that Joaquin Phoenix is his 'favourite actor' and he would love to follow in his footsteps creatively.[45]

* **CHRISTIAN BALE:** Timothée says he was so starstruck when he met his acting hero Christian Bale on the set of *Hostiles* that he was briefly unable to speak![46] Timothée says he asked Bale lots of questions about filming *The Dark Knight*, as well as about his incredible performance in *American Psycho*.

* **TOM CRUISE:** Timothée finds Tom Cruise's work 'inspiring' and admitted that he has watched *Top Gun: Maverick* eight times![47] Timothée got the chance to meet Cruise, and the legendary actor kindly sent him an email with advice on how to prepare for his action-packed role in *Dune: Part Two*.

TIPS FROM TIMOTHÉE

* **DON'T GIVE UP:** After *Interstellar*, Timothée realised his career was not following the trajectory he hoped for as he faced constant rejections at auditions. To this day, he remembers 'the soul-crushing anxiety of feeling like I had a lot to give without any platform' during this period.[48] But Timothée never gave up. He kept working hard and accomplished his dreams.

  What Would Timmy Do? Set clear goals, believe in yourself, and stay disciplined and persistent.

* **NEVER TAKE AN OPPORTUNITY FOR GRANTED:** When Timothée started getting acting jobs, he appreciated every opportunity he received and prepared intensely for each role – no matter how big or small. When Timothée signed up to star in *The French Dispatch*, Wes Anderson sent him an email about how new actors often let him down and 'don't have everything prepared'.[49] So Timothée worked ten times as hard on his supporting role in the film. And when he interviewed Martin Scorsese for GQ, the director couldn't believe it when the conscientious young actor arrived with pages of notes![50]

  What Would Timmy Do? Treat every chance like a (Willy Wonka) golden ticket. Always be ready by learning new stuff and being proactive!

* **KEEP A JOURNAL:** When asked about the best advice he had ever received, Timothée says it was to 'keep a journal'.[51] As well as doing this, he also jots down his thoughts in the Notes app in his phone.[52] He says that the practice helps him have gratitude and appreciation for his life during intense periods of work.

  What Would Timmy Do? Take five minutes each day to reflect on your life and write down something you're thankful for.

Chapter Three

BEAUTIFUL BOY

THE HAIR, THE STYLE, THE ICON

There was a time when Hollywood premieres and awards ceremonies were dominated by male celebrities in predictably boring suits. But, ever since Timothée Chalamet started hitting the red carpet after his breakout role in *Call Me By Your Name*, his bold and fearless approach to fashion has redefined formal dressing for men in the modern age.

Just like the diverse, eclectic and outré roles he plays in his movies, Timothée brings the same range to his red-carpet appearances.

On screen and off, he constantly experiments with fashion, ensuring that no two looks are ever the same, though each is unmistakably his own.

While many of his contemporaries are happy to settle for a standard black tux on the red carpet, Timmy has never been afraid to take risks and blur the lines of genders, genres and eras with his outfits. He has worn everything from a boiler suit (that matched with Zendaya's!) to a sparkly embroidered Louis Vuitton bib and a backless red-hot jumpsuit, infusing excitement and fresh energy into the otherwise monotonous spectacle of male fashion on the red carpet.

TC's politically charged fashion choices strike a chord with a generation that treasures individuality and confidence over homogeneity. Over the years, Timothée has proved himself to be one of the most stylish and boundary-pushing celebrities in the industry – so much so that he was named the 'most influential man in fashion' by *Vogue* at the end of 2019.[1]

'I'VE ALWAYS LOVED THE IDEA THAT YOU CAN APPROPRIATELY EXPRESS YOURSELF THROUGH CLOTHES.'[2]

Perhaps the most intoxicating element of Timothée's style, though, is the fact that he genuinely loves fashion and uses it as a form of self-expression. In fact, unlike most stars, Timothée doesn't employ a celebrity stylist. Instead, refreshingly, he picks all of his red-carpet outfits himself.

'I hear about celebrities who have stylists, and that blows my mind,' Timmy explained to *Time Out* in 2018.[3] 'It's certainly not why I act, but I can wear cool clothes from some of the nicest designers in the world. [So why] am I going to pay someone to figure out what I should be wearing? That's the fun part.'

Let's revisit some of Timothée's most daring and unforgettable outfits and discover what makes him such a fashion icon.

TIMOTHÉE'S STYLE EVOLUTION

THE BREAKOUT WHITE TUX

Timothée still vividly remembers the experience of wearing his first red-carpet outfit. He was going to attend an *InStyle* event for the Screen Actors Guild Awards in January 2013 after being nominated along with the rest of the actors in *Homeland* for the Best Ensemble Cast Award. Still a high-school student, Timothée was planning to go in sweatpants to the awards ceremony. However, upon hearing this, his *Homeland* co-star Morgan Saylor was horrified. Before the awards ceremony, she sent him a text message saying: 'You cannot come in sweatpants, you know this is like a formal thing.'[4] So, at the last minute, Timmy decided to wear a pair of black leather trousers and a black shirt with a rose-coloured tie that he had worn to his high-school prom the year before![5]

Four years later, *Call Me By Your Name* was released to critical acclaim. Timothée's career started reaching new heights and, simultaneously, so did his style. He started slowly but surely building his fashion presence on the red carpet. He wore bold colours for his media appearances for *Call Me By Your Name*, donning a bright-blue suit to a premiere of the film at the Toronto International Film Festival in September 2017,[6] before rocking a burgundy velvet bomber jacket to attend the BFI London Film Festival one month later.[7]

At the age of 22, Timmy would be nominated for an Academy Award for his performance in *Call Me By Your Name* – making

him the youngest Oscar nominee in almost 80 years. He stepped onto the Oscars red carpet in a crisp white tuxedo and bow tie designed by the then Berluti creative director Haider Ackermann.[8] Tim was introduced to Ackermann by the actress Tilda Swinton.[9] Following their first meeting, Ackermann selected this Berluti fitted ivory suit especially for Timothée. 'He was the young dude between all those massive actors. I wanted him to be pure,' Ackermann said.[10] Timothée's tux was a hit with fashion critics. The suit was described as feeling as fresh and youthful as the actor himself.

Timmy's ivory tux put him on the map as one to watch on the fashion scene. It would also mark the start of a creative partnership and 'beautiful friendship' between Ackermann and Timothée.[11] Going forward, Tim would turn to the designer time and time again to create his most audacious and fabulous outfits on the red carpet.

WHO IS HAIDER ACKERMANN? Timothée describes Haider Ackermann as 'one of my closest friends and a creative from a lost era'.[12] A Colombian-born French fashion designer, he is known for his clothing's innovative tailoring and androgynous aesthetic. Ackermann served as creative director of Berluti for three seasons until 2018. Following this, he focused primarily on crafting bespoke red-carpet outfits for celebrities such as Timothée and Kylie Jenner. In May 2024, Ackermann was announced as the parka brand Canada Goose's first-ever creative director.[13]

THE GLITTERY BIB

For the premieres and press calls for his next film *Beautiful Boy*, Timothée would begin tapping into his feminine side with a series of floral suits. He wore a black suit adorned with white flowers to the screening of *Beautiful Boy* at the Toronto International Film Festival in September 2018.[14] One month later, Timmy pulled off an Alexander McQueen graphic pink-and-black floral-printed suit for the London premiere of the film.[15] Fashion enthusiasts were thrilled by these unexpected floral suits. Tim was already establishing himself as someone who was interested in dismantling aesthetic notions of masculinity.

Then, in January 2019, Timothée became a bona fide fashion darling. He showed up to the Golden Globe Awards in an all-black ensemble accessorised with a Louis Vuitton sparkly 'embroidered bib'.[16] The accessory and the outfit had been designed by the late Virgil Abloh, who had then been newly appointed as the creative director for Louis Vuitton. Critics praised Timothée for the gutsy outfit. However, there was a little online confusion over the accessory. Some social media users misidentified the sequinned bib as a 'harness', which is an accessory typically associated with the BDSM and leather scenes.

Timothée famously had to clear up the rumours on *The Ellen DeGeneres Show*. 'I thought it was a bib, they told me it was a bib!' he declared.[17] When he wore the outfit, Tim said he didn't know what a harness was, and he was embarrassed to discover that viewers thought that the bib accessory could have a sexual meaning. Regardless, critics loved Timothée's commitment to bold fashion choices.

In October 2019, TC would sport another glittery look at the London premiere of the film *The King*. He wore a sequinned navy velvet hoodie designed by Virgil Abloh for Louis Vuitton.[18] The sweater was embroidered with more than 3,000 Swarovski crystals and 15,000 sequins. In an interview on the red carpet, Timothée admitted that the sequinned jumper was a 'little itchy',[19] but sometimes you have to suffer for fashion!

'YOU CAN BE WHATEVER YOU WANT TO BE. THERE ISN'T A SPECIFIC NOTION, OR JEAN SIZE, OR MUSCLE SHIRT, OR AFFECTATION, OR EYEBROW RAISE, OR DISSOLUTION, OR DRUG USE THAT YOU HAVE TO TAKE PART IN TO BE MASCULINE. IT'S EXCITING. IT'S A BRAVE NEW WORLD.'[20]

THINK PINK

While on the promotional tour for *Little Women* in December 2019, Timothée was feeling pink! He wore a series of pink outfits, which included a magenta Stella McCartney suit to the premiere of the film in Paris.[21] Timothée also attended a photo call for *Little Women* in London wearing a pale-pink corduroy suit designed by Thom Browne, paired with limited-edition Prada × Adidas sneakers.[22] Timothée seemed to be sartorially addressing *Little Women* with his pastel attire and androgynous tailoring at his press appearances for the film.

In *Little Women*, Timmy starred as Laurie, the childhood friend of Jo March, who is played by actress Saoirse Ronan in the film. According to *Little Women*'s costume designer Jacqueline Durran, Timothée was heavily involved in the styling of his character in *Little Women*.[23] They both wanted Laurie's costumes to defy traditional gender norms and have more feminine qualities. In the movie, Laurie and Jo frequently swap clothes – reflecting Timothée's fashion-forward and gender-blurring choices in real life.[24]

SWEATPANTS AT THE MET GALA

In September 2021, Tim officially got the seal of approval from the most powerful woman in fashion, *Vogue* editor-in-chief Anna Wintour. The then-25-year-old Timothée served as a co-chair at Wintour's Met Gala – becoming the exclusive event's youngest ever co-chair.

And Timmy turned heads when he showed up in sweatpants to the most glamorous fashion soirée of the year.[25] He wore an all-white ensemble by Haider Ackermann, which consisted of a satin tuxedo jacket with black lapels, paired with baggy white sweatpants and Converse sneakers. He also wore a vintage pin and brooch by Cartier, both from the 1920s.

It was a bold style statement that fused TC's love of relaxed and refined aesthetics. Once again, Timothée was embracing risk-taking dressing and redefining men's formalwear. Perhaps Timothée also remembered his first ever red-carpet appearance eight years before and wanted to prove that sweatpants could be high fashion!

GOING SHIRTLESS

In March 2022, Timothée attended the Academy Awards and turned up in a brilliant outfit that further disrupted the fashion world.[26] The actor wore a sparkly cropped jacket overlaid with shiny lace from Louis Vuitton's 2022 spring womenswear collection with black trousers and absolutely no shirt underneath. Skipping a shirt, Timmy instead wore Cartier jewels, including a chain with a charm in the shape of a tiger's head.

Timothée's shirtless look completely broke the rules of red-carpet dressing, and the internet went wild for his outfit. At the time, the *Guardian*'s Alyx Gorman called it 'the biggest fashion moment' of the Oscars that year.[27] Gorman added: 'Not since Jennifer Lopez wore *that* Versace dress to the Grammys has bare décolletage warranted so much discussion.'[28]

THE BOY IN THE RED JUMPSUIT

By 2022, Timothée had proved that his sense of style was groundbreaking. But he would wear his most talked-about and daring red-carpet outfit to date at the *Bones and All* premiere at the Venice Film Festival on 3 September 2022.

Timothée donned a custom jumpsuit with a backless red halter top – which was specially designed for him by Haider Ackermann (who else?). The ensemble featured side slits on the torso, making it sleeveless and nearly backless, with a wraparound, scarf-like neckline. Timmy paired the outfit with black pointed-toe boots, Ray-Ban sunglasses and black rings to match.

Once again, Timothée proved that formal looks do not have to rely on conventional male shirts and jackets. The boldly backless outfit was a defining look for him, with GQ describing it as 'everything we've come to expect from the Timothée Chalamet Red Carpet Experience™: bold, fun, attention-getting, and never too self-serious'.[29]

Then, a few weeks later, Timothée made history as the first man to appear solo on the cover of British *Vogue*'s print edition. He wore a pearl necklace in the cover shoot styled by then-editor Edward Enninful.[30]

In his editor's letter for the issue, Enninful wrote that TC was the unquestionable choice to be British *Vogue*'s first solo male cover star, adding that the fashion world is leaning towards genderless expression and 'dressing to make yourself feel good'.[31] And Timothée embodies that zeitgeist completely.

Tim has continued to redefine the standard men's suit with his red-carpet appearances since then – whether that be the sheer, beaded Tom Ford tank top he wore to the *Wonka* premiere in Paris,[32] or the metallic Haider Ackermann trousers he donned to the London screening of *Dune: Part Two*. No one does it quite like Timmy. As *Vulture* declared, at this point: 'It's Timothée Chalamet's Red Carpet to Lose.'[33]

TIMOTHÉE'S STYLE INSPIRATIONS

Timothée has revealed that he doesn't have any style icons per se, 'because he just likes what he likes and wears what feels right'.[34] But there are a few people who have inspired Timothée's fashion choices.

- **KENNY 'THE JET' SMITH:** In *Elle*'s 'Ask Me Anything' video with his *Dune: Part Two* co-star Austin Butler, Timothée revealed that his style icon is basketball analyst and *Inside the NBA* host Kenny 'the Jet' Smith.[35] 'I feel like [Kenny] has varying style, but he's also very bold and confident about when he just wants to rock sneakers with a suit. And I admire that,' Timothée explained.[36] Kenny could very well be the inspiration for Timothée's love of sneakers on the red carpet. (Meanwhile, Austin Butler revealed that his style icon is Timothée. Cute!)[37]
- **ZENDAYA:** Timothée says that Zendaya has inspired his looks for premieres, especially in terms of wearing an outfit that reflects the themes of the movie that he is promoting.

'I think Zendaya is a great example in this day and age of how you can sort of lean into what the vibe of the movie is in the commercial stuff you do,' Timothée explained. For example, Timothée's iconic blood-red jumpsuit at the *Bones and All* premiere felt like a possible nod to the gory nature of the cannibal movie. Meanwhile, Timothée and Zendaya wore matching futuristic boiler suits to the *Dune: Part Two* press conference in Seoul, South Korea, in February 2024.[38] The pair's coordinated jumpsuits were designed by South Korean fashion brand Juun.J and perfectly embodied the sci-fi genre of the *Dune* movies.

* **HARRY STYLES:** When Timothée wore a floral Alexander McQueen suit to the London premiere of *Beautiful Boy*, he revealed that Harry Styles had inspired the choice.[39] Timothée and Harry have both been credited with promoting a new mode of masculinity with their style, so it's no wonder Timothée admires Harry's aesthetic.

THE HAIR

When Denis Villeneuve took on the colossal task of directing Timothée as Paul Atreides in the *Dune* films, he claimed that the actor himself wasn't the biggest challenge he faced in production. The biggest obstacle he faced in bringing Frank Herbert's sci-fi novel to the screen was managing Timothée's iconic hairdo. 'I had to direct Timothée – and had to direct his haircut,' Villeneuve joked at a Venice Film Festival press conference in September 2021.[40] He humorously remarked that Timothée's hair was 'alive'.[41]

Villeneuve's words are hilarious because they ring true: Timmy's shiny mane is practically its own living entity. While his glorious halo of curls certainly adds to his charm as an actor, Timothée's wondrous hair has become a cultural phenomenon in its own right.

Timmy's frequent co-star and close friend Saoirse Ronan admits she can't go anywhere without being subjected to questions about the actor's epically good hair. 'I'm very used to answering questions about Timothée's hair from 15-year-old girls,' she joked in an interview in 2020.[42]

TC's lustrous mop of perfectly dishevelled curly hair has become a signature part of his image – and his secret weapon. Forget his undeniable talent, Timothée's tresses are unmatched and the envy of fashion journalists everywhere. GQ called it 'once-in-a-generation hair'.[43] While the *Cut*'s beauty director Kathleen Hou declared: 'I don't begrudge Timothée Chalamet his talent, but give me his hair.'[44]

There is also something deeply authentic about Timothée's effortlessly wavy hair, which makes it even more endearing. He has embraced his natural and slightly unruly curls, rather than heavily styling or taming them.

THE HAIRCUT THAT LAUNCHED A THOUSAND TEARS

Needless to say, Timothée's trademark heartthrob hair is a central part of his charm. However, in September 2019, Tim did the unthinkable and chopped off his hair for his lead role of King Henry V in the Netflix movie *The King*. To channel the fifteenth-century monarch, Timothée had to drastically cut his mop of curls into an infamous acorn-style bowl cut. Understandably, Timothée's die-hard fans were devastated. Why would he get rid of his most iconic asset?

It turns out that the man himself was also seriously panicking about his extreme bowl haircut for *The King*. 'Even Timothée was worried,' the film's make-up and hair designer Alessandro Bertolazzi said.[45] But according to Bertolazzi, TC realised that this unsightly hairstyle was 'perfect for the character' of King Henry V in the medieval war saga.[46] The movie hinged on the historically accurate details, which included the type of haircut a young royal would sport in 1413.

After filming *The King*, Timothée said he was relieved when his bowl haircut eventually grew out,[47] but looking back, he says that this memorable hair upset was actually a formative experience for him. It taught him that looks aren't the most important thing and that basing one's self-worth on your appearance is problematic. All in all, he became a little less self-conscious about his hairdo. 'You know, that's the big lesson of life. For things like hair or personality, no one cares,' he said afterwards.[48] However, Timothée did admit to amassing 'an extraordinary hat collection' to hide his embarrassing hairstyle while he was shooting the movie![49]

PERFECTLY IMPERFECT

Although Timothée has never undergone a transformation as drastic as the bowl haircut he had for *The King*, he has sported different hairstyles in some of his other movies. He chopped his hair into a 1980s-style mullet and dyed it a vibrant red colour for the cannibal romance *Bones and All*. Meanwhile, when he starred as rebellious student activist Zeffirelli in Wes

Anderson's *The French Dispatch*, Timothée's wild curls were styled so high that they seemed to defy gravity, reflecting the character's lofty ideals. Then, when the actor took on Roald Dahl's famed avant-garde chocolatier Willy Wonka in the film *Wonka*, Timothée had an artfully wild and unkempt tousled look. *Tatler* hailed Timothée's hairstyle in *Wonka* as the male It boys' equivalent to the coveted 'Rachel' haircut popularised by Jennifer Aniston in *Friends*.[50]

While Timothée's amazing head of hair can largely be attributed to the fact that he won the genetic lottery, he also credits his mysterious hairdresser 'Jamie' for keeping his locks in top shape. 'You know Jamie actually has all the secrets … about my hair,' TC told *Vogue*,[51] referring to his enigmatic and discreet hairdresser, Jamie Taylor. Well known for her expertise with men's hair, she has become the go-to groomer for celebrities like Tim's *Dune: Part Two* co-star Austin Butler and Jared Leto. Jamie says she loves the untamed and unruly nature of Timothée's hair: 'Flaws and little imperfections are perfection to me.'[52] In Timothée's unruly curls we trust!

STYLE LESSONS FROM TIMOTHÉE

- **BE FEARLESS.** Channel your inner Timothée and be confident in what you wear. Timothée's red-carpet looks, like his metallic trousers and sequinned hoodies, show that being bold and self-assured can make a big impact. Start small with a few bold choices of clothing and let your confidence grow!

- **BREAK THE RULES.** Fashion is supposed to be fun, not stuffy, so enjoy it. TC's playful approach is a perfect example of that. He wore sweatpants to the Met Gala, after all! Mix and match different styles and ignore rigid rules to create outfits that make you smile.
- **CREATE A MOOD BOARD.** Gather your favourite Timothée Chalamet looks and create a mood board. Use Pinterest, cut clippings from magazines or print out photos. This visual collection will inspire you and help you pinpoint your style preferences. Tim's eclectic style can spark ideas for your own fashion journey.
- **WORK WITH WHAT YOU HAVE.** Get creative with your existing wardrobe. Timothée is known for reimagining classic pieces with a twist. Use accessories like scarves, belts and jewellery (or a Louis Vuitton sparkly bib if you have one!) to refresh your look and see your clothes in a new light.
- **EXPRESS YOURSELF.** Rocking daring outfits is all about expressing your unique self. Use fashion as a way to express who you are, and don't be swayed by trends that don't resonate with you. Your genuine style will always be in vogue. Timothée always wears what he loves. Follow his lead by staying true to yourself.

Chapter Four

DUNE YOU LOVE ME

LESSONS IN LOVE FROM TIMOTHÉE

When Timothée Chalamet burst onto the scene with his impossibly good looks (and his peachy turn) in *Call Me By Your Name*, he captured our hearts immediately and we were forever obsessed. He became the stuff of instant fandom, and it seemed like the world descended into the throes of full 'Chalamania'. There were suddenly endless fan-made videos dedicated to his iconic dance moves in *Call Me By Your Name*. Meanwhile, the Instagram account @chalametinart went viral by Photoshopping his pretty face onto famous works such as Michelangelo's *David* with the tagline: 'Proof he really is a masterpiece.'[1] Timothée was the heartthrob we had all been waiting for. He was the antidote to the outdated Marvel-superhero brand of masculinity we had seen too many times. And in no time at all, he was the Internet Boyfriend Supreme. But Timothée's overwhelming allure isn't just to do with his looks. We love him for his sweetness, his sensitivity and his obvious emotional intelligence. He seems like a genuinely thoughtful and caring person who is not afraid to show his true emotions. So what do we know about the loves that Timothée has had in his own life? And what can he teach us about love?

'I FEEL LIKE I'M HERE TO SHOW THAT TO WEAR YOUR HEART ON YOUR SLEEVE IS OK.'[2]

THE LOVES OF HIS LIFE (SO FAR)

Timothée may be the most indisputably charming pin-up of our time, but he wasn't always so smooth. And he's not afraid to admit as much, either. His first kiss was lovably awkward to say the least. Timothée revealed that he was 'so nervous' that the girl would be able to tell it was his first kiss, and he kept putting Burt's Bees chapstick on his lips, thinking she would want him to have soft lips.[3] When they finally did smooch, he described himself as 'a total sh*t show'![4]

Timothée may have been happy to share the details of his embarrassing first kiss, but this is a rare insight into his romantic history. He has otherwise always been extremely private about his love life. In fact, when he was asked to reveal his first celebrity crush in a press interview for *Little Women*, he refused to name the star in question.[5] All Timothée revealed was that his first celebrity crush had 'an early 2000s vibe'. Fans have since speculated that it might have been his *Little Women* co-star Emma Watson. Timothée once shared that he grew up avidly watching Emma in the *Harry Potter* movies and he became very flustered when he met her for the first time on the *Little Women* set.[6] He amusingly described the meeting with Emma as 'a weird moment' and it required 'tons of therapy' to get over.[7]

While Timothée may be tight-lipped about his relationship history, it's well known that he dated singer Madonna's daughter Lourdes Leon in 2013 while they were both students at LaGuardia High School of Music & Art and Performing Arts in New York City. Eight years later, Lourdes, who is now a singer and model, reflected on their past relationship and called Timothée 'my first boyfriend'.[8] She fondly looked back at their time together and continued to hold Timothée in high regard. 'I respect him a lot,' Lourdes shared.[9] And it appears that despite the end of their romantic relationship, Timothée and Lourdes remained firm friends. When *Call Me By Your Name* came out in 2017, Timothée revealed that he was still very much in touch with his ex-girlfriend. He said that Lourdes was 'very excited' to see the movie and that she playfully 'teases' him about his newfound fame and public appearances.[10]

In October 2018, Timothée started publicly dating actress Lily-Rose Depp after the pair met while working on the movie *The King* together. In the film, Lily-Rose starred as Catherine of Valois, who is wed to King Henry V of England, played by Timothée. Lily-Rose, who is the daughter of actor Johnny Depp and French singer Vanessa Paradis, was raised in France as well as the US. And just like Timothée, she is fluent in both French and English!

During their relationship, which lasted until April 2020, Timothée and Lily-Rose were photographed sharing a romantic kiss in the rain in New York, and seen sweetly walking arm in arm during a holiday to Paris.

Timothée and Lily-Rose chose to keep their relationship private and away from the spotlight. When Harry Styles interviewed Tim (while he was dating Lily-Rose) for *i-D* magazine, the singer asked him if there was one person he could talk to for the rest of his life.[11] While he confessed that he had 'a clear answer in my head', Timmy opted to keep the person private (personally, we think the answer was Lily-Rose!).[12] Lily-Rose was also politely evasive when pushed to talk about their relationship in red-carpet interviews, although she did praise Timmy's 'incredible emotional capability' in one interview – perhaps a clue as to why she fell for him![13]

However, despite being so protective of their privacy, about a year into their relationship, Timothée was about to find his romance with Lily rudely plastered across gossip sites. In September 2019, he was photographed awkwardly making out with Lily-Rose on a yacht in Capri, Italy. The paparazzi pictures went viral and Timothée (in particular) became the butt of online jokes and memes. Many online commentators suggested that the couple had staged the photos for publicity. In October 2020, after his relationship with Lily-Rose had ended, Timothée reflected on how he was left feeling humiliated by this highly publicised moment, and at being cruelly mocked for his love for his then girlfriend. 'I was on this boat all day with someone I really loved, and closing my eyes, I was like, indisputably, "That was great,"' Timothée recalled. 'And then waking up to all these pictures, and feeling embarrassed, and looking like a real nob.' Timothée couldn't believe that anyone would consider the photos to be a PR stunt and asked: 'Do you think I'd want to look like that in front of all of you?'[14]

After his break-up with Lily-Rose, Timothée started dating *Baby Driver* actress Eiza González. He was photographed kissing Eiza during a beach getaway to Mexico in June 2020.[15] They were also spotted going for a hike together in Los Angeles a few days later.[16] While neither Timothée nor Eiza ever confirmed their relationship, they reportedly split not long after.

Next, Timothée would embark on a relationship that would be highly publicised – no matter how much he tried to keep it out of the spotlight. In April 2023, rumours started to emerge that he was dating none other than Kylie Jenner after the pair met at Paris Fashion Week earlier that year. As the *Telegraph*'s Guy Kelly commented, the unlikely pairing of Timothée with a Kardashian billionaire put the tabloid media 'in a frenzy' and sent social media 'utterly beserk'.[17]

But despite the massive burst of attention about the new It-couple, Timothée and Kylie kept their relationship seriously low-key. They were spotted going to a taco spot,[18] and Kylie was seen driving to and from Timmy's house a few times[19] – once for a family barbecue with his sister Pauline in attendance.[20] Timothée once revealed that he found the term 'date' to be a 'scary word' because it makes people act differently.[21] And

from the looks of it, Kylie's and Timothée's hangouts seem extremely unpretentious, relaxed and down-to-earth – perfect for actually getting to know another person without the scariness of a formal 'date'!

But then, in September 2023, Timothée and Kylie effectively hard-launched their relationship when they were photographed kissing and hugging at Beyoncé's *Renaissance* World Tour show in Los Angeles.[22] Later that month, the pair watched the US Open together and Kylie accidentally revealed that the lock screen on her phone was a photo of Tim kissing her cheek during Milan Fashion Week.[23]

Still, the couple kept shtum about their relationship – even in the face of Kylie's ex-boyfriend Travis Scott appearing to diss Timothée and his *Wonka* role in his track 'Meltdown'.[24]

In January 2024, however, Timothée attended the Golden Globe Awards with Kylie and he could no longer escape the speculation surrounding them. At the awards ceremony, his *A Rainy Day in New York* co-star Selena Gomez was filmed allegedly telling her friend Taylor Swift that Kylie had barred her from taking a photo with Timothée. The footage literally broke the internet and put his relationship with Kylie front and centre before the public. As a result of the scandal, Timothée was chased down by a photographer who interrogated him about the Golden Globes incident, but Timothée kept his cool throughout and calmly said that he, Kylie and Selena were fine. 'We're all good,' he told the paparazzo.[25] Selena also denied the claims.[26] After years of unwanted media scrutiny over his personal life, Timothée has learned how important it is to rise above the gossip.

LOVING TIMOTHÉE

Celebrities, they're just like us! Timothée has not only won our hearts; his unstoppable charm has enchanted numerous legendary stars, too. Here are just some of the luminaries who have also crushed hard on Timmy.

- **Millie Bobby Brown.** The *Stranger Things* star has gushed over Timothée. In an Instagram Live back in 2021, Millie said that her crush was Timothée. She recalled watching one of his movies on a plane and becoming instantly infatuated. 'I think I was crushing on his talent,' she enthused.[27]

- **Jennifer Lawrence.** Three years before they starred together as love interests in *Don't Look Up*, Jennifer Lawrence openly gushed about her attraction to Timothée. She described the actor as 'so hot' and joked that she was going to date him one day.[28] 'I'm going to swing right in there as soon as he's, like, 30,' Jennifer teased back in 2018.[29]

- **Emma Chamberlain.** The ultimate Timothée celebrity fangirl may just be YouTuber Emma Chamberlain. In 2020, she was asked who her celebrity crush was, and she immediately answered: 'We all know who it is. It's Timothée Chalamet.'[30] Emma confessed that she would watch Timothée's movies when she was single to motivate her to meet someone like him. 'He was, like, my muse because I had to, like, fill a void before I found another guy to date,' Emma recalled.[31] Emma's ex-boyfriend Role Model also humorously revealed that he would help her search for Timothée at celebrity parties because Emma was so obsessed with him![32]

- **Glenn Close.** Veteran actress Glenn Close has made no secret of her love for Timothée. The 77-year-old has posted several photos of her and Timothée hanging out together on Instagram, saying he is 'as adorable as he is talented'.[33] The internet went wild for Glenn and Timothée's friendship and dubbed the pair 'Glennothée'.[34]

* **Greta Gerwig.** It is perhaps no surprise that *Lady Bird* and *Little Women* director Greta Gerwig has fangirled over Timothée, too. She says she clocked that he was 'a dreamboat' on their first meeting.[35] When asked to describe Timothée, Greta said: 'Imagine a young Christian Bale crossed with a young Daniel Day-Lewis, with a sprinkle of young Leonardo DiCaprio. Then raise them speaking French in Manhattan and give them a Mensa-level IQ and a love of hip-hop.'[36] Swoon!

HEARTBREAK

In a 2017 interview with the *Guardian* for *Call Me By Your Name*, a 21-year-old Timothée was asked whether he had ever been heartbroken like the movie's character, Elio Perlman.[37] According to the publication, Timothée sighed, leaned forward, clasped his hands and responded: 'I have experienced heartbreak but not in a classical sense.'[38]

While he hadn't suffered heartache in real life at the time, Timothée lives his art, and during his interviews for *Call Me By Your Name*, it became clear that the self-searching Timothée had learned a lot about heartbreak and love through his experience playing Elio. In *Call Me By Your Name*, Elio realises that he should not bury or be ashamed of his feelings after the pain of first love; he should feel them fully. Heartbreak teaches Elio what it means to love and feel truly alive – a powerful experience that should be embraced rather than minimised.

Upon being questioned about his insights from filming *Call Me By Your Name*, Timothée gave a perfect answer. He said: 'The first lesson would be, when you love, love wholly, love unabashedly, give yourself. To suffer is right and if you are feeling, in any kind of way, sh*tty or bad when you're suffering, or you're in heartbreak, or grieving, you're doing it the right way!'[39]

In other words, heartbreak makes us human and that's a comforting thought. Timmy advised other young people going through a break-up to embrace their feelings: 'Nurture your pain, don't extinguish it.'[40]

Timothée also got philosophical about the lessons in love that came about after filming *Bones and All*. The film tells the story of cannibal outcasts Lee and Maren as they embark on a road trip across the US – during which they fall in love and eat humans to survive. Maren and Lee fall in love with each other because, as cannibals, they know what it's like to feel isolated. The pair can accept each other completely for who they are. However, love is scary because it requires them to be emotionally vulnerable and honest with one another.

When Timothée was getting ready to film *Bones and All* at the height of the COVID-19 pandemic, his beloved grandmother passed away. He says he struggled with the feelings of grief over his grandmother's death and being isolated from his family during the pandemic: 'It was a crisis for me.'[41] However, he channelled these real feelings of loss and isolation into filming *Bones and All*, commenting that the film taught him the fearlessness involved in love and how human connection can help us understand our place in the world.[42] 'Without sounding cheesy, I think love is the opposite of fear, the opposite emotion,' Timothée revealed during an interview for the film. 'At least for me. And I really like that.'[43]

BOOKS, FILMS, MUSIC AND ALL

Timothée has always known that art has a profound ability to teach us about the nuances of relationships, love and the human experience in general. Here are some of Timothée's favourite books, films and songs, which have deepened his understanding of the 'mystery of love'.

- ***THE PERKS OF BEING A WALLFLOWER* BY STEPHEN CHBOSKY:** Timothée says that this coming-of-age novel 'took hold of me as a book'.[44] *The Perks of Being a Wallflower* tells the story of Charlie as he navigates his freshman year of high school and his budding sexuality, and struggles to understand the nature of love in all forms.
- ***BLUE VALENTINE*:** When Timothée was asked what film made him fall in love, he responded with the 2010 movie *Blue Valentine*.[45] The largely improvised and unscripted film, which stars Ryan Gosling and Michelle Williams, chronicles the decline of a once-loving relationship. Timothée described *Blue Valentine* as 'such a poignant movie' for its portrayal of a relationship 'falling apart naturally over time'.[46]
- ***PUNCH-DRUNK LOVE*:** Timothée says if there was only one movie that he could watch for the rest of his life, it would be *Punch-Drunk Love*. The film follows an entrepreneur with social anxiety, played by Adam Sandler, who falls in love with his sister's co-worker. The movie demonstrates how love can be transformative, helping people confront their vulnerabilities and grow.[47]
- **'SAD PEOPLE' BY KID CUDI:** Timothée loves this song so much that he sang it on the French television show *Quotidien* in September 2021.[48] On 'Sad People', Timothée's close friend (more on that later!), rapper Kid Cudi, explores the thoughts that plague him at night and his search for

inner peace. Despite his anguish, Kid Cudi sings about how he continues to push himself to realise his dreams.

- **JAMES WHITE:** Timothée says that *James White* is one of his favourite movies of all time and 'a testament to filmmaking'.[49] The movie follows the hedonistic James White, who has to take care of his mother when she is diagnosed with a terminal disease. The movie explores how love can involve facing difficult realities, which can be demanding but also profoundly meaningful.

TIMOTHÉE'S TRIBE

Timothée knows that romantic love isn't the only way to find meaning in life; he cherishes his friendships deeply, too. With his intense career filming movies all around the world, he is always travelling and is sometimes never in the same place for too long. But Timothée says he has made meaningful friendships and met like-minded people all around the world. He revealed: 'I've found my tribe in New York, in Europe, even in Jerusalem. It's been important for me to understand that there are many people like me in the world.'[50]

Finding your tribe is important because it provides a sense of belonging and emotional support. Timothée says that his own friendships have helped him find his identity and stay grounded. He explained that growing up can be tough, but if you can 'find the good people in your life, those non-toxic a*s people,' life becomes a lot less challenging and a lot more fun.[51]

KID CUDI

One of Timothée's closest friends is the rapper Kid Cudi. Growing up, Timothée described Kid Cudi as his favourite artist and 'personal god'.[52] (Funnily enough, years later in 2018, Kid Cudi would tweet that Timothée was his favourite artist.[53] Life really came full circle for Timothée!)

Timothée shared how he and his musical hero became friends. It all started when Timothée got the opportunity to spend a few hours backstage with Kid Cudi at his concert in Montréal, Canada. At the time, Timothée was struggling with breaking into acting after *Interstellar*. Kid Cudi gave Timothée some advice about his professional crisis. The rapper told Timothée about his own emotional lows and the determination that helped him to realise his dreams as a rapper. Timothée says he was so inspired by Kid Cudi's words of advice that he immediately ran home so that he could write down everything he'd said. Timothée still keeps the notes of his first conversation with Kid Cudi on his phone today![54]

By 2019, the pair were fast friends. Timothée was one of only three friends (along with Pete Davidson and Kanye West) whom Kid Cudi invited to his thirty-fifth birthday in Nobu in Malibu.[55] Timothée and Kid Cudi have also supported each other creatively. Timothée performed the opening intro at Kid Cudi's set at ComplexCon in Long Beach, California, in November 2019.[56] The rapper and the actor also appeared together in a hilarious *Saturday Night Live* sketch called 'Weird Little Flute' in April 2021.[57]

In September 2023, there were rumours circulating online that Timothée and Kid Cudi were feuding, but the rapper put the unfounded gossip to bed, tweeting: 'Timmy is my brother til the end of time and beyond[.] I will always ALWAYS love him. We are good. Trust me.'[58]

HIS CO-STARS

Timothée has spoken about how difficult it can be to maintain a friendship with people he has met on movie sets. He shared: 'You just don't stay in touch with everyone, it would just be impossible … It doesn't mean you don't like the other people, but it's just very hard.'[59]

Despite the challenges of his demanding career, however, Timothée has remained close friends with some very special co-stars. One relationship that has persisted over the years is Timothée's friendship with *Chilling Adventures of Sabrina* actress Kiernan Shipka. Timothée first met Kiernan on the set of the 2015 film *One & Two* when they played siblings with supernatural powers. They both spent one month together isolated in South Carolina to film the movie and it resulted in a deep bond. Kiernan says that Timothée is like 'a brother' to her and basically a part of her biological family at this point. 'He's such a part of the Shipka clan. He should hyphenate his last name, actually,' Kiernan once joked.[60] Timothée detailed how he is so close to Kiernan's family that her mother even drove him to his final callback for *Beautiful Boy*.[61]

Timothée Chalamet also counts Saoirse Ronan as a close friend. Timothée and Saoirse first met on the set of *Lady Bird* in 2017 and instantly clicked. In fact, they had such a strong bond that they acted in two more movies (*Little Women* and *The French Dispatch*) together afterwards! Timothée says that he is so comfortable in Saoirse's company that it doesn't feel like a job when they act together.[62] He also said he would love for her to direct him in a movie.[63] Saoirse has even revealed her adorable nickname for Timothée. 'Want to know what I call him? "Pony", because he'll come up to Greta [Gerwig] and me and nuzzle us.'[64]

Perhaps Timothée's most famous and legendary BFF from a movie set, though, is his *Dune* co-star Zendaya. Zendaya says she immediately knew she was going to be 'besties' with Timmy because they shared the same sense of humour.[65] Additionally, Timothée and Zendaya realised they were the only actors of a similar age on the set of *Dune* – the rest of the cast were at least a decade older than them![66] Zendaya says that Timmy would always cheer her up after a long shoot – he would arrive on the *Dune* set with a speaker and they would have 'dance parties' together.[67] Zendaya also helped Timothée set up his first apartment in New York. She took him on a shopping trip to the store Bed Bath & Beyond and got him 'all the big-boy stuff' that he needed in his apartment.[68] Timothée says that Zendaya is 'one of the most grounded people' he knows and 'it's reassuring to have a friend like that' in the entertainment industry.[69] Timothée is also great friends with Zendaya's boyfriend, *Spider-Man* actor Tom Holland. They are so close that Tom called Timothée live on-air during a game of 'Sit Down, Stand Up' on BBC Radio 1 in February 2022.[70]

All in all, Timothée shows that working with someone creatively can sometimes be the best way to forge a long-lasting friendship.

TIMMY'S LESSONS IN LOVE AND FRIENDSHIP

- **EMBRACE YOUR EMOTIONS:** Just like Timothée, don't be ashamed of your feelings. It's OK to feel sad or vulnerable sometimes – these emotions are just as valid and significant as happiness and excitement. Emotions are part of the journey. In fact, embracing your different feelings makes it easier to move forward with a clearer mind and a healed heart.
- **RISE ABOVE GOSSIP:** Ignore the noise and stay above the drama. Your relationship is yours alone. Outside opinions are just that – outside. Your relationship is a bond between you and your partner, not the entire world. So make sure your happiness and connection come first.
- **VALUE YOUR FRIENDSHIPS:** No matter how busy life gets, make time for your friends. Timothée's friendships are as important as his career – balance is everything. Surround yourself with grounded and positive people who uplift you. Friendships make life's adventures more fun and memorable.
- **LEARN CONTINUOUSLY:** Just as Timothée learns from his roles, continually learn about yourself. Emotional growth is a lifelong process. Timothée's passion for films, literature and art also deepens his understanding of love. Dive into the arts to explore different facets of love, heartbreak and relationships.

Chapter Five

CALL ME BY MY NAME

THE UNDENIABLE AUTHENTICITY OF TIMOTHÉE

While Timothée Chalamet is undoubtedly a very attractive man (see entirety of the last chapter) and clearly a very talented actor (see Chapter Two), there have been many other attractive, talented actors in Hollywood who haven't had this kind of Chaleffect. His looks and acting ability can't be the answer alone to Timmy's enormous popularity and devoted fanbase. No, the answer lies in the man behind the jawline. The guy with a poetic, romantic sensibility and open nature.

Self-effacing, sweet, funny and entirely genuine, Timothée is the guy you wished lived next door (your own personal Laurie – although, unlike Jo, you'd definitely say 'yes'). And he is actually someone you could imagine living next door to you, chatting over the fence to you and being exactly the same as the TC you see on chat shows or joking with reporters on the red carpet. Whether you're a fan who's lucky enough to have met him or not, you can be sure that if you did, he would be as you would expect. We've heard this time and time again from those who know him.

This authenticity isn't an accident; Timmy has put in the work to ensure he remains the guy he always was, who can't believe his luck to land each role he does or to continue on the path he's on. In this chapter, we will look at the ways in which Timothée has

'TIMOTHÉE IS A THOUGHTFUL, POETIC SPIRIT. I AM ALWAYS IMPRESSED BY HIS BEAUTIFUL VULNERABILITY.'

DENIS VILLENEUVE[1]

kept himself on the straight and narrow path and the advice he's taken to heart from his mentors along the way.

A TALE OF TWO CITIES: UNDERSTANDING TC'S IDENTITY

Part of what makes Timothée so unique is how he reflects on his own identity, seeking to understand himself better. Part of this involves considering his dual nationality.

Born and bred in New York, he regularly refers to the role his beloved city has played in shaping who he is. As he said in his *Saturday Night Live* monologue in December 2020, 'No matter where I go, I'll always be a New York City kid at heart.'[2] In his acceptance speech at the Gotham Awards in 2017 (when he won Breakthrough Actor for *Call Me By Your Name*), he acknowledged the crucial role the city had played in his success. After stating, 'I'd take a moment to thank some New York artists that have inspired me to pursue this crazy career in the arts,'[3] he named talent as diverse as Mary J. Blige, Al Pacino, Greta Gerwig and Cardi B. He believes the city gave him a huge leg-up with his career, recognising how much harder it can be to 'make it' if you're not from a similar centre of industry. This is part of the reason he respects Kid Cudi so deeply, who is from Cleveland.

He's also recognised that his background has helped him to stay grounded – likely in contrast to growing up LA, where it is famously easy to lose yourself in the false glamour and 'hot air' that gets blown around by agents and executives. To keep his feet on the ground, he says, 'I spend as much time in New York as possible.'[4]

On the other hand, Timothée shared in 2017 that he was still working through his relationship with his French heritage. He said that his time in France as a child had led to 'a little bit of ambiguity in the self-identity sense, which helps a lot creatively because I don't feel as constricted by who I am'.[5] This is perhaps even more the case considering his mum is half Russian Jewish and half Austrian Jewish. This fluidity appears not only in his boundless creativity, but in his persona more broadly – he is a hard guy to pin down! Many who saw *The King*, for example, were convinced he was British and were shocked to later see him speaking with an American accent!

But in 2023, he said in an interview with *Dazed* that he now felt more connected to French culture than he had as a kid, when he'd been drawn to more stereotypical American habits. He said there was a 'stark contrast between the self-empowerment of the United States … versus how things are done in France, where it felt like there was such respect for time, tradition and conversation'. During the pandemic he'd spotted a table of four people deep in conversation, with a receipt sitting next to them that had clearly been there for hours. This had struck him as remarkable, considering that in LA meals are rapid and to the point – over in 45 minutes.

'America is ahead of the times and trendsetting in many ways,' he said, 'but at the same time France has fashion, self-expression and identity that clashes beautifully with a very traditional French passive way of life. I've come to realise and embrace these contradictions of each culture and within myself.'[6]

A 'NORMAL' BOY

When Jimmy Fallon asked Tim whether success had changed him, after a string of hit films had catapulted him to fame in 2018, the young actor answered incredulously, 'How could I change, man?'[7]

Refinery29 hit the nail on the head when recognising that outside of movies TC is 'the ideal boy next door', adding that 'his real life presence can be summarized by another [word]: normal'.[8]

This charming normality seems to be largely due to his commitment to remaining grounded, with Tim almost shrugging off the fact that he's one of the most successful Hollywood actors working today. There is an innate boyishness to him that interviewers continually pick up on – the *Guardian* described the exuberance of a 'bright-eyed and milk-faced' Tim, and how, 'unable to say "um" or "er" without making it sound emphatic', he hooted with joy in response to something Steve Carell had said.[9]

And Tim is very much in on the joke – on *Saturday Night Live* in 2023, he mocked his youthful appearance and young aura when he took the lead in a song with the lyrics 'I got a baby face, but I'm hung like my dad'.[10] Indeed, he's very good at laughing at himself – just check out the video of him falling off his chair at a Q&A for *Call Me By Your Name*! He hilariously jumps up with his arms in the air like a champion, knowing just how to run with the joke, and has everyone in the room shaking with laughter. He later admitted there was a girl in the audience he was 'super-psyched' was there and then he had embarrassed himself in front of her.[11] But we're sure it just made her fall even more in love with his goofiness.

His normality is also evident in his humble demeanour and unpretentiousness. On chat shows, he is almost incredulous about his success and the direction his life has taken. In a particularly memorable Jimmy Fallon interview, he expressed disbelief at the group of amazing actors nominated for a Golden Globe alongside 'little old me'.[12]

In his *TIME* profile interview in 2021, he shrugged off his success, saying, 'It's a combination of luck and getting good advice early in my career not to pigeonhole myself.' He said the term *movie star* is 'like death' to him, and he repeats to himself, 'You're just an actor. You're just an actor!'

On another occasion, when asked why he seems so confident when acting but so nervous on talk shows, he said, 'I think poison for young people publicly, in social settings or in life in general, is self-assumption, and I think that's what makes me nervous on talk shows.'[13] He is acutely aware of how he is perceived by others and can't imagine anything worse than being seen as arrogant.

'BEING VULNERABLE IS NOT A WEAKNESS, NOT A SOCIAL BARRIER. IT DOESN'T MEAN YOU'RE CRAZY OR HYPER EMOTIONAL, YOU'RE JUST HUMAN ... HUMANS ARE COMPLEX; WE NEED TO FEEL A LOT OF THINGS. WE ARE NOT HOMOGENEOUS.'[14]

In 2017, when Matthew McConaughey interviewed Timmy, the two spoke at length about fame. The experienced actor advised Tim, 'You can't be too impressed by it. We have to be respectful of it, but there's a difference between respect and reverence.' Tim said for him that it's all about 'staying present, in that wave'.[15] While McConaughey talked of spending years trying to understand what his own relationship with success might look like, Timothée (perhaps because of having such wise mentors like McConaughey and Steve Carell, as well as, of course, his mum) had a remarkable grasp on things at such a young age.

The internet was pretty much broken (and a lot of dreams came true!) when Harry Styles interviewed Timmy for *i-D* magazine in 2018. Parallels have been drawn between the two many a time, in their deep-rooted authenticity and unwillingness to ascribe to traditional concepts of masculinity.

They're both certainly pushing boundaries in terms of what they wear and how they present themselves – it's no wonder that their fandoms overlap.

One thing that came out of this remarkable interview was that they are both journal keepers. As Timothée said, 'Gratitude and appreciating where you are is very important to me, but that comes with time.'[16] They discussed how important it is to take time to self-reflect and not get lost within the noise – and also simply remember all the amazing experiences that come with the sort of success they've both enjoyed – they don't want to forget any of it. Timmy has said the practice of keeping a journal has helped him to keep within the healthy boundaries he's set himself.

JOURNAL LIKE TIMMY

Take a leaf out of Timmy's book and spend a few minutes each day reflecting on the things that have made you feel good and what you're grateful for. Whether you're a naturally sunny person or someone who needs a little help staying positive, it is widely recognised that this practice helps to boost one's mood.

You can buy yourself a gratitude journal, or just grab a notebook and think about these prompts (opposite). Some of them may not feel applicable every day, but if you keep trying to follow them you may find you're putting yourself into situations that are beneficial – such as getting out to enjoy nature or ensuring you interact daily with someone you care about.

- **Reflect on a kind gesture.** Write down something that someone has done for you today, or something you have done to make someone else's day a little better. How did this make you feel.
- **Appreciate a simple pleasure.** Describe a simple pleasure you experienced today, like enjoying your favourite snack or hearing a song you love.
- **Gratitude for health.** Think about an aspect of your health that you appreciated today and explain why.
- **Acknowledge personal strengths.** Identify a personal strength or skill you used today and how it benefited you.
- **Cherish today's memory.** Recall a happy moment from today. What made it special and why are you grateful for it?
- **Be thankful for relationships.** Write about an interaction you had today with someone you care about. Why are you grateful for this person?
- **Celebrate daily achievements.** List a small achievement or task you completed today and why it made you proud.
- **Nature's wonders today.** Describe something in nature you appreciated today, like a cool breeze or the sound of birds, and why it brought you joy.
- **Appreciation for today's learning.** Reflect on something new you learned today. How has it enriched your life or perspective?
- **Express gratitude for today.** Think about one thing from today that you are thankful for and explain its significance.

TIMOTHEE AND HIS FANS

Timothée's authenticity is evident in his interactions with fans – indeed, there are so many videos of him laughing and joking with them, or stories of TC going out of his way for fans, that it's hard to know where to start! But what is very noticeable is just how tactile he is with them, always offering a hug or an arm around the shoulder for a photo. The amount of love for him, consequently, is so intense that it even has its own name: Chalamania! And there are a huge number of fan accounts you can follow online.

These are just a handful of ways he's made fans feel special:

- As part of a world tour promoting *Call Me By Your Name* in 2018, Timothée and his co-star Armie Hammer danced with fans in the streets of Crema (where some of the film was shot) to 'Love My Way' by the Psychedelic Furs. This incredible moment was cooked up by the duo – Hammer put the message out on his socials, 'Crema … see you at midnight' and 'Anyone with speakers and booze get hugs'. Fans flocked to the square and many videos attest to the incredible moment when the pair, along with director Luca Guadagnino, jumped out of a car and danced with their waiting and utterly jubilant fans.[17]

✳ In 2019, @alankruthahaha (aka Alankrutha) posted an epic thread about her experience sitting next to TC on a plane (in economy, no less!) on a three-hour flight, during which the two shared a long conversation. She wrote, 'What shocks me the most is this dude wanted to know about me. He asked me what I do, what project management is about (literally who cares Timothée), where I grew up and PRONOUNCED MY NAME RIGHT …

his questions were super sincere and genuine and he KEPT high fiving/friendly nudging and while my heart was exploding, I also spoke to him like I would to a friend only bc he made me feel so comfortable![18] He even offered to FaceTime Steve Carell for her and then offered a selfie at the end of the flight!

- In the same year, Tim surprised fans at the premiere of *The King* in a big way! He had tweeted the news that he would be in NYC for the event two weeks prior, and a fan with the handle @eliochalamets replied with the request that Tim bring bagels to the premiere. Somehow Timothée saw it, despite the tweet only getting 77 likes, and initially replied 'lol imagine' – but then he deleted his reply, possibly because he was hoping for the element of surprise, which came on the day of the premiere, when TC turned up with armfuls of his favourite bagels for the fans who had queued up for hours to see them – as one fan said, 'And they were BIG BAGELS!! like the GOOD ones.'[19]
- Tim has been known to remember fans when he's met them before. Not only does this prove he has an excellent memory, but that he considers each and every fan worthy of his full attention each time he meets them.
- Timothée likes to make a fan's day when he can – one video that did the rounds on TikTok featured him approaching a fan in Japan who was holding a sign that read 'I've waited for 9 years to see you' and gifting her a signed Wonka Xbox! That must certainly be a memory she'll hold close forever.

* He is often gifted special handmade presents from fans and shows immense gratitude whenever this happens. Many have commented on the time he's taken looking at them and even showing particularly special ones to his family members or whoever he is with at the time. He is also often gifted peaches, which he receives with good grace (if a little embarrassment!).

FAMILY MATTERS

A huge key to Timothée's level head and inner strength comes from the unwavering love and support of his family. It certainly helps that they understand something of the world he's moving in now, with his mum's background as a Broadway performer, his dad's work in the media and his sister's career as a successful actress.

So much more important than this, though, is that he knows how proud they are of him and that they will always stand by him. He says he feels the full weight of this pride to such an extent that he *almost* finds it almost overwhelming – but 'in a great way'.[20] He's said this doesn't make him feel any pressure, as this pride is not tied to him winning awards or scoring great parts, but by being who he is and taking such pride himself in what he does. Although he did joke, '[My awards] are weirdly, like – they're my mum's now. And they're with all my childhood taekwondo trophies.'[21]

He is also incredibly close with his sister, Pauline. She has been quoted as saying she's 'in awe of the work that he does and the projects he works on', just as her brother 'has come to almost every screening of a short film I've written or directed or acted in'.[22] #siblinggoals

Timmy has frequently brought his family with him to big events like awards shows and premieres, and they look on, beaming, as he does his 'Timothée Chalamet' thing! In his words: 'I think the most precious thing I get from my parents – and I try and give it back to them as much as I can – is their love and support.'[23]

THE PRINCIPLES TIMOTHÉE LIVES BY

Timothée certainly feels things very deeply and is a very principled guy, and, not one to virtue-signal, he lives by the values he cares about, allowing his choices or film roles to speak volumes.

Here are just some of principles or causes TC holds dear:

- **LGBTQ+ RIGHTS:** Despite being straight (as far as we know), Timothée has embraced his queer-coded image, which was cemented after his role in *Call Me By Your Name*. He is

regularly hailed as a queer, bisexual or even lesbian icon, and earned himself the unofficial title of 'Hollywood's Straight Prince of Twinks'. When an interviewer from *Out* magazine asked him about his feelings towards this designation, and being so beloved by the queer community, he was visibly pleased. He said that he'd hoped the film would help people understand this 'version of love' as something not niche or persecuted, but 'just a thing'.[24] Seeing something is, of course, the best way to normalise it. He has also shown support to the community in other ways, such as donating money to New York's LGBTQ+ centre.

'IN A POST #METOO WORLD, TIMOTHÉE CHALAMET REPRESENTS THE CHANGE WE WANT TO SEE IN THE FILM INDUSTRY. HE'S SENSITIVE, HONEST, THOUGHTFUL, POLITE, GOOFY, AND SELF-AWARE. HE'S IN TOUCH WITH HIS FEMININE SIDE, AND HE SMILES. A LOT.'

I-D [25]

- **FEMINISM AND THE REJECTION OF TOXIC MASCULINITY:** Tim tirelessly champions the women in his life and his co-stars, as well as fanboying over his favourite artists like Cardi B and Mary J. Blige. But the biggest impact he has had is through his rejection of traditional masculinity – in his sartorial choices (see Chapter Three), the roles he's played and how he's embraced vulnerability. He and Harry Styles have been at the forefront of a perceptible cultural shift. But Timmy has once again put his money where his mouth is on this cause. As discussed in Chapter Two, when the #MeToo movement hit its zenith and brought about a resurgence of interest in the historic sexual abuse allegations against Woody Allen, *A Rainy Day in New York* was nearing completion – the film directed by Allen and starring Timothée Chalamet. Tim responded to the scandal by speaking publicly about his remorse for taking the role and donated all of his wages for the film to three charities, including Time's Up, a non-profit organisation raising money for victims of sexual harassment.
- **THE NEED FOR POLITICAL ENGAGEMENT IN YOUNG PEOPLE:** When Harry Styles asked Tim whether he felt the pressure to be political, he responded that it wasn't pressure but a 'responsibility', that complacency in previous generations has caused a lot of problems today, but that he's pleased young people are more engaged now.[26] He also expressed admiration for young people standing up for what they believe in, including Emma González, who survived the Parkland school shooting in Florida,

2018, and has become a gun-control activist. He made his political leanings very clear on Instagram ahead of the 2020 election, when he urged his followers to help vote Donald Trump out.[27]

- **THE FIGHT AGAINST CLIMATE CHANGE:** Timothée's role in the film *Don't Look Up* clearly pointed to his concern about the public's apathy about what mankind is doing to the planet, but his lifestyle choices serve to reinforce this message. He is a great believer in sustainable fashion, regularly wearing and championing clothes and accessories by ethical fashion designer Stella McCartney, vegan footwear brand Tretorn and items from LOEWE's Eye/LOEWE/Nature range, the Spanish label's sustainability-focused sub-brand, crafted from recycled, organic polyester. As Timothée knows only too well: you are what you wear!

- **ADDICTION AWARENESS:** When promoting *Beautiful Boy*, Timothée always focused the conversation on the subject matter of the film itself, even though interviewers would lead by complimenting his performance. He has described how much time and energy he spent getting to the heart of understanding addiction and the impact this horrible illness can have. He said the role 'stayed with me longer than I thought it would', and that after he finished filming he 'still felt really affected, drained and a little devasted'.[28] Even though the movie itself is redemptive and hopeful, getting to the heart of what addiction can do to lives was very emotional for him, and he made it his mission to speak up about the issue as much as he could.

He described in interviews how addiction is an illness that doesn't discriminate and no one's life is immune from its far-reaching impact. Breaking the taboo was very important to him and was why he chose to take this part in the first place – although he felt huge pressure to play this crucial role well. I think we can all agree, he smashed it!

THE FACTS MAKETH THE MAN

When getting to the heart of Timothée's authenticity itself, it's useful to understand more about his tastes and passions. Here are a handful of facts you won't find anywhere else in this book that may help you to understand him a little better!

- If Timothée could only listen to one song for the rest of his life, it would be 'Rain' by Kid Cudi.
- Tim described his happy place as a summer's day in New York.
- Timmy is an excellent pianist – he took lessons for *Call Me By Your Name* and in the film he performs a complex piece, the *Allegro* from J.S. Bach's Capriccio in B flat major. The piece is subtitled 'On the Departure of a Beloved Brother', as the young Bach wrote it for and dedicated it to his sibling.
- TC is able to play the guitar – something he also picked up for his role as Elio in *Call Me By Your Name* – but has had to work on his skills a lot more to play the iconic role of Bob Dylan in *A Complete Unknown*.

- Tim's go-to karaoke song is 'Heart-Shaped Box' by Nirvana, but he is wary of performing it in front of people he doesn't really know.
- His favourite TV show is *The Office*, but Tim has also professed his love for animated TV show *Rick and Morty* and says he was a big *Growing Pains* fan.
- If he could only read one book for the rest of his life, he would choose *The Book of Disquiet*, written in Portuguese originally by Fernando Pessoa.
- Try not to get too excited, but Tim confessed to Harry Styles that he sleeps in the nude!
- As a child, he was a big fan of the Power Rangers and *Yu-Gi-Oh!*
- Timmy is a big football (soccer) fan. Saint-Étienne are his favourite club, but in the Premier League he supports Chelsea. Matt Lucas, who acted alongside TC in *Wonka*, told *The One Show* they weren't able to discuss football together: 'He's a Chelsea fan. Yes [that's a problem], 'cause I'm an Arsenal fan. He loves his football, he knows a lot about it, and when he's over here he does go to some games.'[29]

THE MEANING OF LIFE ACCORDING TO TIMOTHÉE CHALAMET:

'WE'RE ALL ONLY HERE FOR SO LONG. LIVE AND LET LIVE. LOVE DEEPLY. LOVE OPENLY. AND KNOW THAT THE WISE MAN KNOWS HE'S IGNORANT BUT CULTIVATES MORE UNDERSTANDING.'[30]

HOW TO CONNECT WITH YOUR AUTHENTIC SELF

The journey to self-love isn't always the easiest one, but it is certainly one worth committing to. Using Timothée Chalamet as inspiration, here are some tips on how to embrace authenticity on your personal journey:

- **BE HONEST ABOUT THE THINGS YOU LOVE:** Often, we learn most about ourselves by being truthful about our interests and passions. Never be ashamed about the things you like or the way you think – it's all too easy to get caught up in trying to be 'cool' and falling in line with our peers. Next time you're tempted to do this, think about how Timmy fanboys over the celebrities he admires, waxes lyrical on his passions and speaks out about things he cares about. And millions of people LOVE him for it, clearly seeing his honesty and integrity, which shine through with every syllable he utters.
- **FAME AND FORTUNE ARE NOT PERSONALITY TRAITS:** It's a tale as old as time that a young person finds success and becomes a fame-monster overnight. Recognising that money and celebrity are simply great additions to your life helps you to keep them from becoming central to your identity. Timmy is constantly showing immense gratitude for his success and continually expressing how bizarre his life is right now, so it's likely he'll never take success for granted or let it pull him under.

- **HOLD CLOSE THOSE WHO KNOW YOU BEST:** Throughout our lives, we will often make new and exciting friends. That's obviously terrific, and it's always fun to reinvent yourself when you have the opportunity, but it's also important to have people in your life who know you to your core and love you for who you really are. For Timmy that's his family, but for many of us that can be friends we've known for years. If they really love you, they will be open to you changing and growing, but they should be there to help you stay true to who you really are, no matter what life throws at you.
- **EMBRACE VULNERABILITY:** You don't have to be perfect; you just have to be you. Only by allowing others to see you as you truly are can you ever achieve real closeness – whether that's by sharing your fears, hopes, dreams or imperfections.
- **IDENTIFY YOUR CORE VALUES:** Once you understand them, you will be many steps closer to understanding yourself.
- **ALLOW TIME FOR SELF-REFLECTION AND GRATITUDE:** Whether that's through journalling, like Timmy, or simply by spending quiet time thinking, you will only be able to let the authentic you out once you have a true understanding of who that person is.

Chapter Six

A RAINY DAY

COSY UP WITH SOME CHALAMET-INSPIRED QUIZZES

WHICH TIMOTHÉE CHALAMET FILM SHOULD YOU WATCH NEXT?

1. What type of movie are you in the mood for?

A) Drama

B) Romance

C) Coming-of-age

D) Historical

E) Science Fiction

F) Musical

2. You're bingeing on a TV show on Netflix – what it's going to be?

A) *13 Reasons Why*

B) *The Summer I Turned Pretty*

C) *Ginny & Georgia*

D) *The Last Kingdom*

E) *The Expanse*

F) *A Series of Unfortunate Events*

3. What's your favourite thing about Timothée?

A) His ability to explore complex human emotions and relationships.

B) His fluid sex appeal and chemistry with his co-stars.

C) His charisma.

D) His controlled sense of ambition and power.

E) How even as an action hero he is unconventional and interesting.

F) How quirky he is.

4. You've got a free afternoon, you decide to ...

A) Do some journalling for some self-care.

B) Relax in the sun with your latest squeeze and a peach.

C) Call your mum or another family member for a long catch-up.

D) Read a historical book.

E) Go to a martial-arts class.

F) Bake a chocolate cake.

5. What kind of story arc are you interested in?

A) A family dealing with difficult issues.

B) A heartwarming love story.

C) A teenager navigating personal growth.

D) A powerful figure rising to prominence.

E) A hero embarking on an epic journey.

F) A young man with imagination and a dream, battling to make it a reality.

6. How do you feel about film adaptations of books?

A) I love them if they handle sensitive topics well.

B) They are great if they capture the essence of romance.

C) They should stay true to the character's journey.

D) They should bring historical figures to life.

E) They should expand the world and lore of the original.

F) I love an imagined origin story for a classic.

7. Which of these supporting actors are you most excited to see?

A) Steve Carell

B) Armie Hammer

C) Saoirse Ronan

D) Joel Edgerton

E) Rebecca Ferguson

F) Hugh Grant

8. How do you want to feel after watching the movie?

A) Emotionally drained and ready for some introspection.

B) Immensely moved, romantic and wistful for lost loves.

C) Reflective and ready to rebuild bonds with those you love.

D) Roused and thoughtful.

E) Awestruck and eager to watch another.

F) Delighted, enchanted and ready to break into song.

Results

Mostly As: *Beautiful Boy* (2018) You're in the mood for a deep, emotional drama. *Beautiful Boy* follows the harrowing journey of a family coping with addiction.

Mostly Bs: *Call Me By Your Name* (2017) A beautiful and moving love story set in the Italian countryside. This romance will captivate your heart.

Mostly Cs: *Lady Bird* (2017) You're looking for a relatable coming-of-age story. *Lady Bird* captures the trials and triumphs of teenage life.

Mostly Ds: *The King* (2019) If historical dramas are your thing, *The King* offers a gripping tale of Henry V's rise to power.

Mostly Es: *Dune* (2021) You're ready for an epic science-fiction adventure. *Dune* transports you to a fantastical universe with high stakes and breathtaking visuals.

Mostly Fs: *Wonka* (2023) You're in the mood for a musical! *Wonka* will awaken your childhood fantasies, and likely make you fancy some chocolate.

WHICH TIMOTHÉE CHALAMET CHARACTER ARE YOU MOST SIMILAR TO?

1. How would your friends describe your personality?

A) Creative and introspective.

B) Romantic and passionate.

C) Witty and charming.

D) Sensitive and artistic.

E) Adventurous and intense.

2. How would you prefer to spend your weekend?

A) Writing music or poetry.

B) Spending time with a loved one.

C) Exploring the city and trying new things.

D) Relaxing in a beautiful, tranquil setting.

E) Going on a spontaneous road trip.

3. What is your greatest strength?

A) Your creativity.

B) Your loyalty.

C) Your charisma.

D) Your emotional depth.

E) Your fearlessness.

4. How do you handle difficult situations?

A) Reflect on them and find inspiration in the struggle.

B) Rely on the support of loved ones.

C) Use humour and wit to navigate through them.

D) Dive deep into your emotions and express them.

E) Face them head-on and adapt as needed.

5. What is your favourite type of music?

A) Folk and classic rock.

B) Classical and romantic ballads.

C) Jazz and indie pop.

D) Ambient and acoustic.

E) Anything raw and edgy.

6. What is your dream career?

A) Musician or writer.

B) Scholar or artist.

C) Journalist or actor.

D) Photographer or filmmaker.

E) Explorer or chef.

7. How do you express your feelings?

A) Through writing or music.

B) By being open and honest with loved ones.

C) Through humour and conversation.

D) By creating art or being in nature.

E) Through bold actions and spontaneity.

Results

Mostly As: Bob Dylan (from *A Complete Unknown*) You are creative and introspective, finding inspiration in your surroundings and experiences. You have a unique way of seeing the world and often express your thoughts through art or music.

Mostly Bs: Laurie (from *Little Women*) You are romantic and passionate, valuing deep connections with those around you. Loyalty and love are central to your life, and you often go to great lengths to support and care for your loved ones.

Mostly Cs: Gatsby (from *A Rainy Day in New York*) You are witty and charming, with a love for exploration and new experiences. Your charisma draws people to you, and you have a knack for making even the simplest moments feel special and memorable.

Mostly Ds: Elio (from *Call Me By Your Name*) You are sensitive and artistic, deeply in tune with your emotions and the beauty of the world around you. You cherish meaningful experiences and often express your feelings through creative outlets.

Mostly Es: Lee (from *Bones and All*) You are adventurous and intense, unafraid to face challenges and take risks. Your bold and fearless nature drives you to explore new horizons and live life to the fullest, even if it means stepping into the unknown.

TIMOTHÉE CHALAMET: TRUE OR FALSE?

1. Timothée Chalamet was born in France.
2. Timothée's sister is a famous singer.
3. Timothée Chalamet starred in a Christopher Nolan film.
4. Timothée was nominated for an Academy Award for his role in *Beautiful Boy*.
5. Timothée dropped out of Columbia University after only one year.
6. TC won an Oscar for his role in *Call My By Your Name*.
7. Timothée Chalamet's middle name is Louis.
8. *Dune* is based on a sci-fi novel by Philip K. Dick.
9. Timothée Chalamet supports Chelsea football team.
10. Timmy has dated the daughters of Madonna, Johnny Depp and Phil Collins.
11. Joaquin Phoenix is Timothée's favourite actor.
12. Greta Gerwig directed Tim in *Lady Bird*.
13. Tim's karaoke song is 'Smells Like Teen Spirit' by Nirvana.
14. The film that made Timothée want to become an actor was *The Joker*.
15. Tim played Jennifer Lawrence's boyfriend in the film *Don't Look Up*.

Answers

1. False. He was born in New York City, USA.
2. False. She's an actress.
3. True. He played Tom Cooper in *Interstellar*.
4. False. He was nominated for an Academy Award for Best Actor for *Call Me By Your Name*.
5. True. He dropped out to pursue acting more freely.
6. False. He received a nomination but didn't win.
7. False. His middle name is Hal.
8. False. *Dune* is written by Frank Herbert.
9. True. He is a big Chelsea fan.
10. False. He didn't date Lily Collins.
11. True. He has said he would love to follow in his footsteps creatively.
12. True. Gerwig directed him in both *Little Women* and *Lady Bird*.
13. False. It's 'Heart-Shaped Box' by Nirvana.
14. False. It was *The Dark Knight*.
15. True. He was one of a star-studded cast.

COMPLETE YOUR TIMOTHEE CHALAMET BINGO CARD

Simply cross off each box as you complete them to achieve ultimate fandom!

B	I	N	G	O
Read *Little Women* by Louisa May Alcott	Follow Timothée on social media	Watch Lil Timmy Tim's rap video about statistics on YouTube	Read the Wikipedia page on wormholes	Watch one of TC's opening monologues on *SNL*
Master ten new phrases in French (or another European language)	Put his birthday in your diary – 27 December 1995	Eat a peach	Seen *Wonka?* Try watching Gene Wilder in *Willy Wonka and the Chocolate Factory*	Maybe you've watched *The King* – how about the Shakespeare play *Henry V?*
Craft something out of chocolate	Commit to no more fast fashion	Go for a walk in the rain	Follow a Timothée Chalamet fan page	Listen to a best-of Bob Dylan playlist
Watch a TC film in the place it was filmed – maybe Lombardy (CMBYN), or London (*Wonka*)!	Watch a Chelsea football match	Do a detailed drawing of a ladybird	Donate to an addiction support charity	Read *Dune* by Frank Herbert

NOTES

INTRODUCTION

1 Sam Lansky, 'Timothée Chalamet Wants You to Wear Your Heart on Your Sleeve', *TIME*, 11 October 2021

CHAPTER ONE

1 Matthew McConaughey, 'Timothée Chalamet', *Interview*, 2 June 2017
2 *The Ellen Show*, 'Timothée Chalamet Once Locked his Naked Mom Out on a Balcony', YouTube, 11 January 2019
3 Brianna Holt, '"I planted seeds": Timothée Chalamet's mother on her children's success', *Guardian*, 6 March 2022
4 Savannah Walsh, 'Pauline Chalamet Is Coming of Age, Again', *Vanity Fair*, 18 November 2021
5 Holt (n3)
6 Bwog Staff, 'PeopleHop: Timothée Chalamet', *Bwog Columbia Student News*, 19 September 2013
7 Daniel Riley, 'The Arrival of Timothée Chalamet', GQ, 14 February 2018
8 William Earl, 'Timothée Chalamet Reveals How Heath Ledger's "Dark Knight" Performance Inspired Him to Act', IndieWire, 7 January 2018
9 Merle Ginsberg, 'How "Fame" School Nearly Stifled Timothée Chalamet's destiny', *New York Post*, 19 January 2019
10 Erin Nyren, 'Timothée Chalamet Says He Wanted to Be LeBron James Growing Up (Watch)', *Variety*, 3 January 2019
11 Bwog (n6)
12 *i-D*, 'Timothée Chalamet Meets Harry Styles', *VICE*, 2 November 2018
13 McConaughey (n1)
14 Ibid.
15 Holt (n3)
16 *i-D* (n12)

CHAPTER TWO

1 Jan Janssen, 'Timothée Chalamet on love, loss and isolation in *Bones and All*', Style, 3 January 2023
2 Josh Duboff, 'Meet Timothée Chalamet and Ansel Elgort's High-School Drama Teacher, Mr Shifman', *Vanity Fair*, 19 January 2018
3 *The Ellen Show* (ch1 n2)
4 Crystal Bell, 'Timothée Chalamet is still learning how to be a leading man', MTV News, 27 February 2018
5 Riley (ch1 n7)
6 *Variety*, 'Timothée Chalamet Wept After Watching "Interstellar"', YouTube, 4 December 2018
7 Riley (ch1 n7)
8 *Variety*, 'Timothée Chalamet & Emma Stone | Actors on Actors', YouTube, 5 December 2018

9 Austin Hargrave, 'Timothée Chalamet: I don't how the f**k any of this happened"', *Time Out*, 5 October 2018
10 Ibid.
11 Riley (ch1 n7)
12 Ben Brantley, 'Review: "Prodigal Son," John Patrick Shanley's Exploration of the Student He Was', *New York Times*, 9 February 2016
13 Stephen Holden, 'Review: In "Miss Stevens" a Chaperone Greets Temptation', *New York Times*, 15 September 2016
14 Alison Willmore, 'The Boy King: He could be our next great leading man – if he can figure out what kind he wants to be', *Vulture*, 4 December 2023
15 Julie Miller, 'Inside Timothée Chalamet's Overnight Breakout', *Vanity Fair*, 5 December 2017; Anna Menta, 'Timothée Chalamet on "Call Me By Your Name," Vulnerability and That Peach Scene', *Newsweek*, 24 November 2017
16 Anne T. Donahue, 'Harry Styles proves the heartthrob is dead: long live the artthrob', *Guardian*, 27 September 2016
17 K. Austin Collins, 'Timothée Chalamet Makes the Overwrought *Hot Summer Nights* Worthwhile', *Vanity Fair*, 26 July 2018
18 James Mottram, 'Timothée Chalamet reveals his relationship philosophy: "Love is the opposite of fear"', *Metro*, 30 November 2022
19 Leyla Mohammed, 'Timothée Chalamet's Agent Revealed He Hasn't Auditioned for Anything in Over 7 Years and It's Sparked a Conversation About Nepotism, Privilege, and Industry Connections', BuzzFeed News, 9 January 2023
20 Lynn Hirschberg, 'Timothée Chalamet in Conversation: A Raw, Honest Talk About Addiction, Recovery, and His Film Beautiful Boy', W, 17 January 2019
21 Dino-Ray Ramos, 'Timothée Chalamet Donates Salary from Woody Allen Film to Time's Up, RAINN', Deadline, 15 January 2018
22 Alissa Wilkinson, 'Greta Gerwig's *Little Women* adaptation is genuinely extraordinary', Vox, 20 December 2019
23 *The Tonight Show Starring Jimmy Fallon*, 'Timothée Chalamet on *Wonka* and the *Barbie* Cameo with Saoirse Ronan that Never Happened', YouTube, 14 December 2023
24 Josh Kurp, 'Denis Villeneuve Isn't Sure There Would Be A "Dune" Movie Without Timothée Chalamet', UPROXX, 21 July 2021
25 Jamie Dunn, 'Timothée Chalamet on *The King*, *Dune* and fame', The Skinny, 24 October 2019
26 Zack Sharf, 'Timothée Chalamet: "I Was Blindsided by Massive 'Dune' Production"', *Variety*, 27 October 2022
27 Associated Press, '"Dune is dream come true": Villeneuve, Chalamet over the moon', Daily Sabah, 6 September 2021
28 Brian Davids, 'Denis Villeneuve on "Dune" Success and the Road to "Part Two"', *Hollywood Reporter*, 28 October 2021
29 Zack Sharf, 'Why Wes Anderson Cast Timothée Chalamet: He Belongs in the French New Wave', IndieWire, 16 October 2020
30 'Q&A: Timothée Chalamet on "The

French Dispatch"', *Coup de Main*, 9 December 2021
31 Jon Frosch, David Rooney, Lovia Gyarkye, 'Critics' Conversation: The Great Film Performances of 2022', *Hollywood Reporter*, 6 December 2022
32 Nadia Khomami, '"Societal collapse is in the air": Timothée Chalamet on cannibal romance *Bones and All*', *Guardian*, 2 September 2022
33 Chioma Nnadi, 'Timothée Chalamet on French-Guy Hair, Filming With Scorsese, and Being the New Face of Bleu de Chanel', *Vogue*, 15 May 2023
34 Rhiann Phillip, 'Timothée Chalamet As Wonka Makes Perfect Sense, Actually', *Vogue*, 11 December 2023
35 Hugh McIntyre, '"Wonka" Music Supervisor on Teaching Timothée Chalamet to Sing and the Possibility of a Sequel', *Forbes*, 3 March 2024
36 Danni Scott, 'Second *Wonka* trailer battles more controversy as fans claim another role was "miscast"', *Metro*, 12 October 2023
37 Matthew Velasco, 'Timothée Chalamet Continues to Make Box Office History', W, 18 March 2024
38 Daniel Riley, 'Timothée Chalamet Goes Electric', GQ, 17 October 2023
39 Ethan Shanfeld, 'Timothée Chalamet to Star in Josh Safdie, A24 Movie About Ping Pong Pro (EXCLUSIVE)', *Variety*, 5 July 2024
40 Jaden Thompson, 'Denis Villeneuve and Legendary Developing "Dune 3" and "Nuclear War: A Scenario" Film Adaptation', *Variety*, 4 April 2024
41 *i-D* (ch1 n12)
42 W, 'Timothée Chalamet Talks Hollywood Rejection and Auditioning for "Beautiful Boy" | W Magazine', YouTube, 17 January 2019
43 Build Series, 'Timothée Chalamet & Steve Carell Gush Over Each Other', YouTube, 11 October 2018
44 Amy Nicholson, 'Denis Villeneuve and Timothée Chalamet: "Dune" Dynasty', *New York Times*, 21 February 2024
45 Martha Tesema, 'Frank Ocean interviewed Timothée Chalamet and we don't know who to be more jealous of', Mashable, 6 February 2018
46 Hargrave (n9)
47 Riley (n38)
48 Lansky (Introduction n1)
49 *Coup de Main* (n30)
50 GQ, 'Timothée Chalamet & Martin Scorsese Have an Epic Conversation | GQ', YouTube, 17 October 2023
51 Lynn Hirschberg, 'Timothée Chalamet Things "Date" Is "Very Much a Scary Word"', W, 8 January 2018
52 *i-D* (ch1 n12)

CHAPTER THREE

1 Steff Yotka, 'Timothée Chalamet Is the Most Influential Man in Fashion', ***Vogue***, 18 November 2019
2 'Timothée Chalamet On "Adultifying", Being Back Home in NYC and His Style Icons', *Vogue*, 15 September 2022
3 Joshua Rothkopf, 'Timothée Chalamet: 'I don't know how the f**k any of this happened', *Time Out*, Undated
4 Lynn Hirschberg (ch2 n51)
5 Ibid.
6 'Timothée Chalamet attends "Call Me By Your Name" premiere at

the Toronto International Film Festival', UPI
7 '"Call Me By Your Name" Photocall – 61st BFI London Film Festival, Getty Images
8 Brooke Bobb, 'Timothée Chalamet, Oscars Darling, Continues to Do No Wrong in a White Berluti Suit', *Vogue*, 4 March 2018
9 Khanh T.L. Tran, 'The bromance continues: Timothée Chalamet opts for his favorite label Berluti for the Oscars', *Los Angeles Times*, 4 March 2018
10 Noah Johnson, 'Haider Ackermann Opens Up About Berluti: "I'm Still Close with All My Exes"', GQ, 9 August 2018
11 Nicole Phelps, 'Haider Ackermann – Timothée Chalamet's Closest Fashion Collaborator – Tells All', *Vogue*, 6 December 2019
12 Jerry Stafford, '"You have to protect your future"', *System*, Issue 20
13 Yang-Yi Goh, 'Haider Ackermann, Timothée Chalamet's Fashion BFF, Is Canada Goose's First-Ever Creative Director', GQ, 15 May 2024
14 Christian Allaire, 'Timothée Chalamet Does the Cool Guy's Suit at the Toronto Film Festival', *Vogue*, 8 September 2018
15 Christian Allaire, 'How Timothée Chalamet Pulled Off the Tricky Floral Suit', *Vogue*, 14 October 2018
16 Naomi Pike, 'Timothée Chalamet Was Not Wearing a Harness at the Golden Globes', *Vogue*, 7 January 2019
17 *The Ellen Show* (ch1 n2)
18 Christian Allaire, 'Timothée Chalamet Shakes up the Red Carpet with a High-Fashion Hoodie', *Vogue*, 3 October 2019
19 On Demand Entertainment, 'Timothée Chalamet Talks Sequins, Politics, Brits and The King Henry V Bowl Cut!', YouTube, 3 October 2019
20 *i-D* (ch1 n12)
21 Maria Bobila, 'Timothee Chalamet's Latest Red Carpet Flex? An Eiffel Tower Keychain', *Nylon*, 12 December 2019
22 Erika Harwood, 'Timothée Chalamet Wore a Pink Corduroy Suit, We Repeat, Pink Corduroy Suit', *Nylon*, 17 December 2019
23 Devon Ivie, 'Timothée Chalamet's *Little Women* Outfits Are Anachronistic, Just for His Fans', *Vulture*, 17 December 2019
24 Erica Gonzalez, 'Jo and Laurie Shared Clothes on Purpose in *Little Women*', *Harper's Bazaar*, 9 February 2020
25 Christian Allaire, 'Timothée Chalamet Walked 10 Blocks to the 2021 Met Gala – and Showed Up in Sweats', *Vogue*, 13 September 2021
26 Chelsey Sanchez, 'Timothée Chalamet Isn't Wearing a Shirt Under His Sparkly Blazer on the Oscars Red Carpet', *Harper's Bazaar*, 27 March 2022
27 Alyx Gorman, 'Chest in show: Timothée Chalamet gives 2022's Oscar red carpet its biggest fashion moment', *Guardian*, 28 March 2022
28 Ibid.
29 Sam Schube, 'Timothée Chalamet Goes Backless in Venice', GQ, 2 September 2022
30 Giles Hattersley, 'The Chalamet Effect: Timothée Talks Fate, Fashion and Being an Old Soul', *Vogue*, 15 September 2022
31 Edward Enninful, 'Timothée Chalamet Is British *Vogue*'s First Solo Male Cover Star', *Vogue*, 15 September 2022

32 Melissa Minton, 'Timothée Chalamet shimmers in sheer beaded top on Paris "Wonka" premiere red carpet', Page Six, 1 December 2023
33 Erin Schwartz, 'It's Timothée Chalamet's Red Carpet to Lose', *Vulture*, 6 December 2023
34 Kerry McDermott, 'When Timothée Met Edward: *Vogue*'s October Cover Star Gets Candid Over a Vegan Burger', *Vogue*, 15 September 2022
35 *Elle*, 'Timothée Chalamet & Austin Butler Reveal Wildest Headlines About Themselves | Ask Me Anything | *ELLE*', YouTube, 22 February 2024
36 Ibid.
37 Ibid.
38 Matthew Velasco, 'Zendaya & Timothée Chalamet Go Full Wonder Twins', W, 21 February 2024
39 On Demand Entertainment, 'Timothée Chalamet inspired by Harry Styles', YouTube, 13 October 2018
40 Joe Utichi, 'Denis Villeneuve's Biggest Challenge On "Dune"? "Dealing with Timothée Chalamet's Hair. It's Alive." – Venice Film Festival', Deadline, 3 September 2021
41 Ibid.
42 Daniel Riley, 'The Making (and Remaking) of Timothée Chalamet', GQ, 15 October 2020
43 Garret Munce, How to Get Timothée Chalamet's Epically Good Hair', GQ, 15 February 2018
44 Kathleen Hou, 'Why Is Timothée Chalamet's Hair So Great?' *The Cut*, 12 March 2018
45 Samantha Sasso, 'Timothée Chalamet Wasn't Sure About His Bowl Cut in *The King*, Either', Refinery29, 3 October 2019
46 Ibid.
47 *Late Night with Seth Meyers*, 'Timothée Chalamet on 'The King' and Meeting Co-Star Emma Watson', YouTube, 1 November 2019
48 Ibid.
49 Ibid.
50 Chandler Tregaskes, 'Is the "Wonka" the new "Rachel" for It boys? Timothée Chalamet's hairdresser tells all to *Tatler* – and reveals how to recreate *that* artfully tousled Willy-esque look', *Tatler*, 20 December 2023
51 Hannah Coates, 'Meet the Stylist Behind Timothée Chalamet and Austin Butler's Heartthrob Hair', *Vogue*, 9 June 2023
52 Ibid.

CHAPTER FOUR

1 Caroline Goldstein, 'A Viral Instagram Account Is Inserting Actor Timothée Chalamet into Historical Paintings – and the Results Are Hilariously Convincing', Artnet, 18 July 2018
2 Lansky (Introduction n1)
3 *W* Magazine, 'Timothée Chalamet on His Funny First Kiss | *W* Magazine', YouTube, 15 December 2023
4 Ibid.
5 Associated Press, 'First Celebrity Crush: Pugh and Chalamet', YouTube, 14 February 2020
6 YouTube (ch3 n47)
7 Ibid.
8 Britt Hennemuth, 'Lourdes Leon Is Ready to Express Herself', *Vanity Fair*, 21 April 2021
9 Ibid.

10 SiriusXM, 'Timothée Chalamet's First Time Meeting Andy Cohen', YouTube, 28 November 2017
11 *i-D* (ch1 n12)
12 Ibid.
13 On Demand Entertainment, 'Lily-Rose Depp Reveals What's So Special About her Boyfriend, Timothée Chalamet', YouTube, 3 October 2019
14 Riley (ch3 n42)
15 Kelby Vera, 'Timothée Chalamet, 24, proves he's more than moved on from Lily-Rose Depp as he puckers up to Eiza Gonzalez, 30, during a romantic trip to Cabo... just two-months after news of his break-up with the model', *Daily Mail*, 23 June 2020
16 Bianca Betancourt, 'Timothée Chalamet and Eiza González Reunite in L.A. Following Their Mexico Getaway', *Harper's Bazaar*, 30 June 2020
17 Guy Kelly, 'Does Timothée Chalamet know he's dating Kylie Jenner?', *Telegraph*, 5 September 2023
18 'Kylie Jenner and Timothee Chalamet Low-Key Taco Date in Her Car!', TMZ, 14 April 2023
19 Justin Enriquez, Ashleigh Gray, 'Kylie Jenner and Timothée Chalamet have been "hanging out" at his Beverly Hills home – despite "taking things slow"', *Daily Mail*, 1 June 2023
20 Alyssa Bailey, 'Kylie Jenner and Timothée Chalamet Were Photographed Together and With Their Families for First Time', Yahoo!Life, 1 June 2023
21 Hirschberg (ch2 n51)
22 'Kylie Jenner & Timothée Chalamet: Romantic Night Out At Beyoncé Concert... Lots of Hugs and Kisses', TMZ, 5 September 2023
23 @elle_mexico, Instagram, 21 September 2023: https://www.instagram.com/p/CxdNVpHsP0g/?img_index=1
24 Carlos De Loera, 'Beefing with Wonka? Travis Scott maybe shaded Timothée Chalamet in his new song', *Los Angeles Times*, 28 July 2023
25 'Timothée Chalamet: No Drama Between Kylie, Selena ...Everyone's All Good!!!', TMZ, 9 January 2024
26 @enews, Instagram, 8 January 2024
27 The Tea, 'Millie Shares Her CELEBRITY CRUSH on Instagram Live Stream', YouTube, 11 July 2019
28 *Entertainment Tonight*, 'Watch Jennifer Lawrence Gush Over "So Hot" Timothée Chalamet! (Exclusive)', YouTube, 21 February 2018
29 Ibid.
30 #WomensFashion, '#LouisVuitton Guide: Emma Chamberlain Plays LV Trivia Game with Derek Blasberg | LOUIS VUITTON', YouTube, 17 November 2020
31 Emma Chamberlain, 'How to look cute on your period', YouTube, 14 February 2012
32 GQ, 'Emma Chamberlain & ROLE MODEL Take a Couples Quiz | *GQ*', YouTube, 14 February 2023
33 @glennclose, Instagram, 11 January 2019
34 Hunter Harris, 'Glenn Close and Timothée Chalamet Are Best Friends Now, Can You Believe It', *Vulture*, 14 January 2019
35 *Entertainment Weekly*, 'Greta Gerwig on Casting "Lady Bird's" Rising Stars | Cover Shoot | *Entertainment Weekly*', YouTube, 29 January 2018

36 Brennan Carley, 'Timothée Chalamet on Paparazzi Catching His Kiss with Selena Gomez, *Call Me by Your Name*, and *That* Peach Scene', *GQ*, 20 November 2017
37 Kate Kellaway, '*Call Me By Your Name*'s Oscar-tipped double act on their summer of love', *Guardian*, 15 October 2017
38 Ibid.
39 Editorial Team, '*Vogue Hommes* meets break-out "Call Me By Your Name" star, Timothée Chalamet', *Vogue Hommes*, 5 March 2018: https://www.dailymotion.com/embed/video/x6e4ffu
40 @tchalametdaily, Instagram, 6 April 2020
41 Janssen (ch2 n1)
42 Khomami (ch2 n32)
43 Mottram (ch2 n18)
44 Philip Galanes, 'How to Come of Age Onscreen? Saoirse Ronan and Timothée Chalamet Know', *New York Times*, 31 January 2018
45 Kino TV, 'Timothée Chalamet has a morbid taste in romantic movies', YouTube, 4 June 2020
46 Ibid.
47 *i-D* (ch1 n12)
48 Sandra innit, 'Timothée Chalamet and Denis Villeneuve on *Quotidien* Interview | Sep 07, 2021', YouTube, 7 September 2021
49 'A Day in the Life of Timothée Chalamet', *VMan39*, Spring/Summer 2018; Xavier Dolan, 'Timothée Chalamet by Xavier Dolan', *VMan* interview on Tumblr, 22 February 2018
50 Janssen (ch2 n1)
51 *Glamour* Magazine UK, 'Timothée Chalamet & Zendaya on Friendship, Mental Health & Feeling Different | *GLAMOUR* UK', YouTube, 22 October 2021
52 Riley (ch1 n7)
53 @RealChalamet, X, 27 March 2018
54 Riley (ch1 n7)
55 Michael Saponara, 'Kid Cudi Celebrates Birthday With Kanye West, Pete Davidson & Timothée Chalamet: See Pics', *Billboard*, 31 January 2019
56 Katherine Gillespie, 'Watch Timothée Chalamet Open for Kid Cudi', *Paper*, 4 November 2019
57 *Saturday Night Live*, 'Weird Little Flute ft. Kid Cudi – *SNL*', YouTube, 11 April 2021
58 @KiDCuDi, X, 10 September 2023
59 James West, 'Back in the day with Timothée Chalamet', *Hero*, 31 March 2018
60 Kathryn Lindsay, 'For Kiernan Shipka's Next Trick, She'll Make Sabrina Disappear', Refinery29, 10 February 2020
61 Hirschberg (ch2 n20)
62 David Canfield, 'True Romance: Saoirse Ronan and Timothée Chalamet on reuniting for *Little Women*', *Entertainment Weekly*, 17 October 2019
63 Galanes (n44)
64 Ibid.
65 Christian Holub, 'Doing *Dune* right: Inside the making of the long-awaited (and star-packed) adaptation', *Entertainment Weekly*, 13 October 2012
66 *Glamour* Magazine UK (n51)
67 *The Late Show with Stephen Colbert*, 'Zendaya and Timothee Chalamet Threw Dance Parties on the Set of "Dune"', YouTube, 3 February 2021
68 *Jimmy Kimmel Live*, 'Jimmy Kimmel Interviews Timothée Chalamet, Zendaya, Austin Butler & Florence Pugh', YouTube, 2 February 2024
69 Ibid.

70 BBC Radio 1, 'Tom Holland pranks Andrew Garfield, Timothee Chalamet and Greta Thunberg: Sit Down, Stand Up', YouTube, 10 February 2022

CHAPTER FIVE

1 Lansky (Introduction n1)
2 *Saturday Night Live*, 'Timothée Chalamet Monologue – *SNL*', YouTube, 13 December 2020
3 Gil Kaufman, '"Call Me By Your Name" Star Timothée Chalamet Shouts out Cardi B in Gotham Awards Speech', *Billboard*, 28 November 2017/
4 *i-D* (ch1 n12)
5 Jenna Marotta, '"Call Me by Your Name": Timothée Chalamet is Learning How to Be a Man, Onscreen and Off', IndieWire, 17 November 2017
6 Alex Peters, 'Exclusive: Timothée Chalamet on his French roots and becoming a Chanel boy', *Dazed*, 15 May 2023
7 *The Tonight Show Starring Jimmy Fallon*, 'Timothée Chalamet Reacts to Being Photoshopped into Artwork Memes', YouTube, 11 October 2018
8 Morgan Bailer, 'An Introduction to Timothée Chalamet', Refinery29, 22 February 2018: https://www.refinery29.com/en-us/2017/12/186281/who-is-Timothée-chalamet-actor-call-me-by-your-name
9 Ryan Gilbey, 'Steve Carell and Timothée Chalamet on drugs, disillusionment and playing father and son', *Guardian*, 13 December 2018
10 *Saturday Night Live* (n2)
11 *The Tonight Show Starring Jimmy Fallon*, 'Timothée Chalamet Meeting Angelina Jolie & Jennifer Aniston Back to Back Blew His Mind', YouTube, 11 January 2018
12 Ibid.
13 *i-D* (ch1 n12)
14 Ibid.
15 McConaughey (ch1 n1)
16 *i-D* (ch1, n12)
17 Bridget Read, 'Watch Timothée Chalamet and Armie Hammer Dance in the Streets Where *Call Me by Your Name* Was Filmed with Fans', *Vogue*, 31 January 2018
18 Allie Gemmill, 'A Timothée Chalamet Fan Shared What It Was Like Meeting Him on a Plane', *Teen Vogue*, 6 February 2019
19 Steph Eckardt, 'Timothée Chalamet Distributed Bagels to His Fans at *The King*'s New York Premier', W, 2 October 2019
20 *i-D* (ch1 n12)
21 *The Tonight Show Starring Jimmy Fallon* (n7)
22 Walsh (ch1 n 4)
23 *i-D* (ch1, n12)
24 Rose Dommu, 'Timothee Chalamet on Being Hollywood's Straight Prince of Twinks', *Out*, 16 December 2019
25 *i-D* (ch1 n12)
26 Ibid.
27 Jessica Napoli, 'Timothée Chalamet makes his thoughts on the 2020 election clear', Fox News, 15 October 2020
28 *i-D* (ch1 n12)
29 Apratim Banerjee, 'Timothee Chalamet reveals which football club he supports and sings club's song to bemused Dune cast, video emerges' *Sportskeeda*, 15 February 2024
30 *i-D* (ch1 n12)

PICTURE CREDITS

Alamy Stock Photo: 27/Evan Agostini/ Associated Press, 37/Jordan Strauss/ Associated Press, 41/Alessio Bolzoni/Photo 12, 43/François Duhamel/Photo 12, 45/TCD/PROD.DB, 49/Niko Tavernise/ ©Warner Bros./ Everett Collection, 52/©Warner Bros./ Landmark Media, 61/Anthony Behar/ Sipa US, 66/PA Images, 71/Vianney Le Caer/Associated Press, 73/Lee Young-ho/ Sipa US, 75/Hyperstar, 76/Landmark Media, 87/ PMC, 90/JordonStrauss/ Associated Press, 115/ Album.

Getty Images: 84/Stephane Cardinale-Corbis, 95/John Sciulli, 98/Ethan Miller.

Shutterstock: 19/Everett Collection, 50/Photo Yannis Drakoulidis/© MGM/Everett Collection, 65/Matt Baron/ BEI, 69/Matt Baron, 111/ David Fisher, 113/January Images, 144/Steve Sands/ NewYorkNewswire/Bauer-Griffin.

Illustrations © Ollie Mann